Start Programming Mobile Apps with Android Java

Bill Tait

Contents

1. Start

Android Java

Java is a programming language that is widely used to write software applications for desktop and laptop computers, web servers, web browsers, and Android mobile devices such as phones and tablets. There are even different names for these applications. In mobiles they are usually called apps.

So Java is supposed to be a "write once, run anywhere" language but, of course, that is not really possible because of the huge differences between the platforms. But it does come close, so the language is the same but it has to be adapted to work in these systems.

It is adapted by using an application structure, called a framework, and a set of matching code components. These are specifically designed for each platform. The framework defines how Java is to be used and code components help you to use it.

So if you already know Java you are half way there. Otherwise you may as well just learn Android Java and limit the scope of your ambitions to that particular version, for the time being.

In fact, apps for Android mobile devices are generally written in a mixture of Java and XML. The programs are written in Java and the user interfaces are written in a version of the eXtensible Markup Language, XML. So, Android developers usually have to learn how to write Java and XML. However, it is entirely possible to write Android apps with very little XML and that is the approach adopted here.

The Aim

The book is an introduction to the development of mobile apps for beginners. This means beginners to programming, beginners to Java and beginners to Android. However, learning to program, especially in Java, is not a simple task so the book is certainly not for dummies.

The treatment is designed to be as easy as possible for beginners in a number of ways. First of all it is selective. It does not cover all there is to learn about Android mobile development. In particular, it concentrates on the Android Java language rather than the xml files used in some Android apps to design user interfaces. It is just Java.

It is also just graphics. To get to grips with real apps in a fairly short time the book concentrates on one type of app. All the apps are graphical apps. These are introduced in a progression of increasingly complex projects with Java theory added as we go along.

The ultimate goal is to enable you to read Java code and understand it sufficiently to write your own code and create your own apps, distribute them, and publish them on the Google Play Store.

The treatment is also based on practice rather than theory. The reasoning here is that beginner programmers often find it difficult to drive themselves through long chapters on Java theory without an immediate purpose. So the book concentrates on the development of mobile apps and introduces the theoretical principles on a need-to-know basis, as we go along.

However, the main problem for beginners to Android development is often not the Java language or even the Android peculiarities, but the development environment. We have to use another software application to produce Android apps. This is called an Integrated Development Environment, or IDE, and has to be covered in some detail at the beginning of the book. It allows a developer to write program code and convert it into an app. In this book we will use Android Studio as recommended by Google itself. However, if you are already familiar with one of the alternatives, such as Eclipse, then you can use that since the coding chapters will not be specific to any one IDE.

The apps will be developed progressively by adding increments to each app in order to produce the next one. The final app will be a ball game, called Getball, which is available for free download from the Google Play Store so you can see what the overall aim of the book is. All of the apps can be extended and developed into your own versions which can be published on the Play Store. You are free to use any of the code presented in this book in your own apps.

The Method

There are two mental processes that help people to learn a new subject. One is to think about it and the other is to use it. Educators call these theory and practice. Both are important in learning how to write programs and develop them into apps. We can see them as reading code and writing it.

The approach adopted in this book is to introduce theory and demonstrate the practice in a readable way, as a story. So it is possible to read each chapter without laying a finger on a keyboard.

However, it is not possible to get a full understanding of programming without actually trying it. So in each chapter you are invited to apply what you have learned and do some coding, usually to extend an example or an app in your own way. This will mean copying the code from this book into your IDE then changing it in some way to check that you have really understood it.

To make this easy and, in fact, to follow the general approach to software development, we will always create a new app by extending the previous one. So we develop in relatively small increments from one app to the next. Then, although the program code may become quite long in the later chapters the additions and modifications are quite manageable.

And while you are writing the code it is important to note that the main problem for all novice programmers, and many experienced ones, is typing accurately. Java code is very precise so when you are entering source code you have to replicate every detail including spelling, character case and punctuation.

Android Development

The development environment is a software package that helps you to write and test programs. Mainly it provides a text editor that lets you write program code and helps to keep it correct by highlighting any errors. Then it compiles this source code into an executable program and runs it so that you can test it. The compiling part just translates your work from written English source code to whatever form of binary code is required by the computer system you are writing for. In this case the language is Java and the target is an Android mobile device.

So we are looking for a software product that will help us to write mobile apps, test them and even prepare them for publication on the Google Play Store. And since it will include all these functions in one package, we describe it as an Integrated Development Environment, or IDE.

There are several options for an IDE. The most widely used is probably Eclipse. This is a free, multipurpose application that is used to develop software for various purposes, including Java development, so you may already be familiar with it. For Android it must have the Android Development Toolkit or ADT.

Another option is Android Studio which is more of a dedicated product but similar to Eclipse. Both of these IDEs run on a PC or a Mac or Linux computer and can either simulate a mobile Android device or connect to a real one for testing your apps. However, both are quite complicated to install and use so they are not the ideal starting point for novice programmers.

A simpler alternative is an IDE that runs on an Android device itself. The most widely used of these is probably AIDE. This is an app that runs on an Android device and allows you to develop your own apps and test them on the same device. AIDE stands for Android Integrated Development Environment and it can be downloaded from the Google Play Store. It is best to start with the free version with which you can develop relatively small apps, like some of those developed here, and test them on your mobile device.

Unfortunately, although AIDE is free for small apps it is not for all of the apps that we will develop in this book. It is also somewhat overloaded with ads which can be quite distracting. Also, developing on Android can be a difficult process because of the small screen and the absence of multiple windows which facilitate the copying of code from one app to another.

So in this book we will use Android Studio as our development environment. This is now the standard Android development environment and the only one supported by Google.

Programming for Beginners

Java is not easy to learn and not generally recommended for beginners to programming. This book attempts to make it as easy as possible by being selective and practical as described above, but you may have to persevere to get through it. If you want an easier approach to Android app programming you might have a look at MIT's App Inventor. This uses a visual approach designed for children but used by beginners of all ages. If you want a soft start to programming in general, then MIT again has the answer. This is a package called Scratch. Both of these can be investigated at the MIT web site. Also there is a Google offering in the form of Google Blocky that uses the same visual format.

You can try these packages as preliminary studies to Java, or as alternatives to Java. You might also consider JavaScript, which is a slightly simpler language than Java and can be converted to Android apps with Cordova or Appcelerator Titanium both of which can be found on the web with the usual Google search. But none of these options can match the capability and performance of a Java app. Java is more powerful, it can do more things and it can do them better and faster, so if Android programming is your goal you will have to try Java at some stage.

So here we go with Java but first we will have a quick look at our Development Environment.

2. Development

The IDE

To develop an Android app you need an Integrated Development Environment, that is, an IDE. This lets you write Java code, convert it to an app, then run your app to test it. It lets you start with an idea and end up with an app installed in your Android device.

The first stage of the integrated development process involves writing the Java source code. The IDE should help by highlighting code errors. If there are none, the second stage compiles the source code into the machine code that makes up the app. And the third stage is to test your app. You can do this by running it in a simulated Android device or in a real one connected to your computer.

For this book we will develop on a PC with Android Studio. Also, we will be installing the IDE and developing our apps on a Windows system. If you are using something else the only chapter that will be affected much is this one.

The remainder of the book, apart from the final chapter on publishing, will be relatively independent of the choice of IDE or operating system so if you are using a different system you should have no problems with the coding chapters.

Installing Android Studio

This is probably the most difficult part of the book for beginner programmers but it is an essential part. Android Studio does not (yet, at least) simply install itself on your computer like some other applications. There may be as many as four stages to the installation of Android Studio, as follows:-

- First the latest version of the Java SDK has to be installed.
- The Android Studio package has to be installed
- The Android SDK may have to be updated
- The AVD may also have to be edited.

Installing Java

You need a recent version of the Java SDK installed on your computer to use Android Studio. This is the Software Development Kit, or SDK, not the runtime engine, the JRE or JVM. Incidentally, the same is true if you are using Eclipse with the ADT, plugin.

You can find out if you have Java installed on a Windows system by visiting the Control Panel then choosing the Programs option which should include Java. You may have to do a Google search to find out how to get to the Control Panel on your system or how to see installed programs on a non-windows system. Or, of course, you can find out the hard way by trying to install Android Studio which will fail if there is no Java SDK available.

You can install the Java SDK from the oracle site at

http://www.oracle.com/technetwork/java/javase/downloads

Or search for it yourself.

You should install the latest recommended version of the SDK, such as the 8u31 used here. Click the button to install and accept the license agreement then click on the download option that fits your system. It should take only a few minutes.

Installing Studio

Now download Android Studio from the android website at

https://developer.android.com/sdk/installing/studio.html

As usual, accept the license agreement then run the installer. Accept all the default options to complete the process.

Now run the application. If there is no Java installed or the application cannot find it, you will get an error message to the effect that no JVM is found. You may have to find the environment variables on your system and add a JAVA_HOME variable that points to the JDK directory, such as

C:\Program Files\Java\jdk1.8.0_31

In Windows systems this is in the Control Panel, System and Security, System, Advanced System Settings, Environment Variables. If you are using some other system then, again, you should search for information on how to find the environment variables.

Then the Setup Wizard downloads a few components and we have a welcome screen as illustrated in Figure 1.

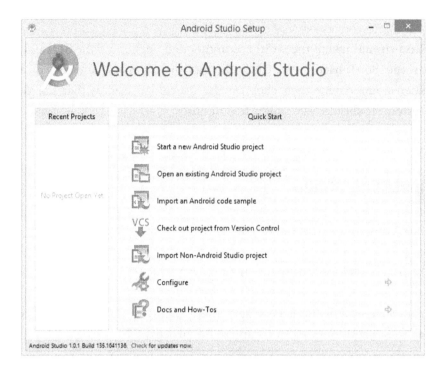

Figure 1. The Android Studio welcome screen.

To test the installation you should choose the option to start a new Android Studio project.

You may be offered a selection of app templates. If so it is best to start with a blank template at this stage. These templates are for different types of Android device and each will provide you with some starting code. The exception is the No Activity template which gives you nothing. So start with the Blank Activity – second from the left.

This will open a second screen as shown in Figure 2.

The Form Factors

You will be asked to choose what types of device you are developing for. The initial choice is in a form such as that described in Figure 2.

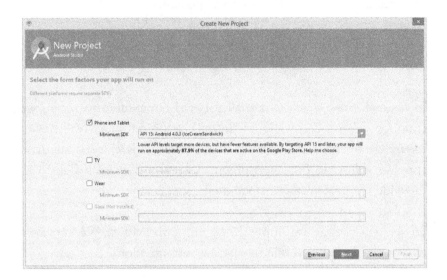

Figure 2. The screen to select the app form factor.

Here the selection has been made for you by Studio. It is for a phone or tablet device with an Android API level of at least 15. If you intend to develop for devices with a lower API then you should select an appropriate value from the drop down list.

Usually Froyo, with an API level of 8, is a safer bet and will be used in the remainder of this book.

An API is an Application Programmers Interface. It is a collection of code components that can be used in the app and is updated regularly. These updates correspond to specific Android versions, which also have their own names, some of which are as follows:

Lollipop	API 21	Version 5.0
Kit Kat	API 20	Version 4.4 and 4.4W
Jelly Bean	API 19 - 16	Version 4.4 – 4.1
Ice Cream Sandwich	API 14 - 15	Version 4.1
Honeycomb	API 11	Version 3.0 – 3.2
Gingerbread	API 9,10	Version 2.3
Froyo	API 8	Version 2.2

In general, these versions are all forward compatible so if you write code for version 2.2 it should run in version 5.0 but it will not take advantage of the newest features introduced in later versions. In our apps we will write for levels down to version 2.2 and make do with the code features available since then.

So we will change the input in Figure 2 to API 8. We can always change this later by editing one of the package files.

Creating a New App

An app is always developed as a project since it consists of several separate files packaged together. So we start the development by creating a new project, as shown in Figure 3.

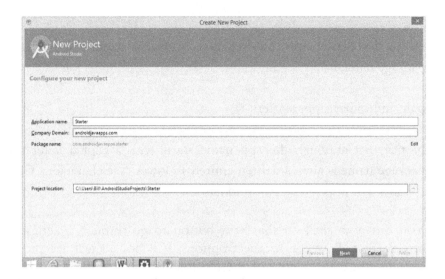

Figure 3. The screen to create a new project.

The first option is the name of your app. We will call our app Starter so that should be entered into the name box.

Then you need to enter a company domain. This is the domain of an assumed developer company. It is added in reverse to the app name to form a package name which is displayed below these two entries. This package name is the full name of your app in the Play Store or on a mobile device, so it has to be unique, that is, different from all the other apps. There may be other apps called Starter but there is no conflict unless the domains are the same. It is like placing files with the same names in different folders of your computer. The company name defines the namespace in which the app exists,

The key to defining a unique package name is to declare a company domain that is uniquely yours. In all of the apps developed in this book we will use the domain androidjavaapps.com. It is important to note that before publishing your apps you must replace this domain with one of your own registered domains.

25

So, in this Starter app the domain is androidjavaapps.com and the package name is

com.androidjavaapps.starter

Notice that although the app name starts with a capital letter the package name is always written entirely in lower case characters. Case is important in Java and Android names.

You can now click on the Next button to go through a series of screens that allow you to select options. It is best to just accept the defaults but make a note of the file folders used since you have to find them outside of Studio. Finally you will be able to click on the Finish button to open the development screen as shown in Figure 4.

In this book we will always use the domain android.javaapps.com, a form factor for a phone and tablet with a Froyo minimum SDK, a Blank Activity, and finally an Activity Name of MainActivity. You can however, give it a different Title in this last page, which will appear as the name of your app

The Development Screen

The screen in which all the development will take place is illustrated in Figure 4. A project consists of a number of files and two of these are listed in the tabs near the top of the screen. These are MainActivity.java and activity_main.xml. The latter is already selected and its contents are displayed in the workspace below.

The activity_main.xml file is an xml file that defines the user interface for your app. It will probably start in the mode shown in the figure, which is the Design mode. This is a graphic representation of the user interface. It shows a phone displaying the present contents of the user interface which is just the simple text message, "Hello world". This has become something of a tradition in computer programming when learning a new language.

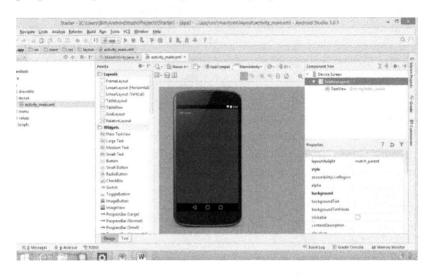

Figure 4. The user interface xml file displayed in Design mode.

At the bottom of this display there are two tabs. The Design tab is presently selected. If you click on the adjacent Text tab the screen will display the same file but in its underlying text mode, which is in the form of an xml file as illustrated in Figure 5.

Figure 5. The user interface file displayed in text mode.

If you are familiar with xml then you should be able to understand this file. If not, don't worry. This book concentrates on the Java content of an Android app and we will not be doing much with this and the other xml files contained in the app. In fact we will ignore the file for the time being.

However, in passing, it is worth knowing that an Android app is actually a collection of files in a single compressed folder. Some of these are xml files and some are java files. Most app developers work on both types but in this introductory treatment we will do almost all of our programming in the java files. We will return to this topic towards the end of the book so that you understand exactly what is going on.

The Project Files

An Android Studio project comprises several files and their organization is, to say the least, confusing. You can view them on your computer or in Studio and if you delete them from the computer they are deleted also from Android Studio.

In the computer they are in whatever folder you selected when you installed and ran Studio. The default, and the one used here is

C:\Users\Bill\AndroidStudioProjects\Starter

You should make sure Users is not a hidden directory since you will want to access it to manage your files. Or, of course, you can choose another, more convenient folder.

The Starter folder corresponds to this particular project and opens up to show a large number of subfolders and some files. We are interested only in one of these subfolders, namely, app. The others, including build and gradle are used by Studio to compile the app and we will not be exploring them. The app folder contains all the files that we are interested in.

- app\src\main\java\androidjavaapps\starter\MainActivity which is our main code file. This folder will also contain other code files that we write.

- app\src\main\res\ which contains a number of resource files used by our app.

- app\src\main\AndroidManifest which defines the complete app and its components

- app\build\outputs\apk\app-debug.apk which is our product, the compiled app file. This is not present until the app has actually been compiled and it always has this name.

These files are imported into the Android Studio workspace and displayed in the left hand pane of the development environment. This project pane shows the files for a single project. If you open another project you have the choice of replacing the current one or using a separate window. So there is only ever one project in each window.

If the project files are not displayed you can click on the side tab to display them. They may display exactly as in the computer file system or they may display in an abbreviated form. This shows only two folders, named app and Gradle Scripts. You can open these to see the contents by clicking on the adjacent triangular icons. Re-clicking closes the folder.

The app folder corresponds to the app folder in the computer file system. Opening this reveals three subfolders, called manifests, java and res. The first contains only one file, AndroidManifest.xml. The java folder contains two subfolders both named after the app. The first one contains MainActivity and any other java files we write. The last of the three java subfolders, res, contains the resources used by the app.

Then double clicking on a file name opens it in the central workspace area alongside any other files already there. Each has a tab at the top

of the workspace so it can be selected for display and editing by clicking on the tab. Or it can be removed from the workspace by clicking on the tab close icon.

The Starter Code

We have just created an app called Starter and this is currently showing in the development screen. The main Java file, MainActivity.java is already open in the workspace and all we have to do to view it is to click on its tab. However if it is not already open then it can be found in the projects pane at

app/java/com.androidjavaapps.starter, or

app/src/main/java/com.androidjavaapps.starter

Double clicking on this name opens the file in the workspace pane where we can edit it and develop our app. We can also close the xml file which we will not be using. So the environment is now as illustrated in Figure 6.

Figure 6. The working layout of Android Studio.

Default code is generated by the IDE for whatever form factor you selected. If that was the blank activity the code is as follows:-

```java
package com.androidjavaapps.starter;
import android.support.v7.app.ActionBarActivity;
import android.os.Bundle;
import android.view.Menu;
import android.view.MenuItem;

public class MainActivity extends ActionBarActivity {

    @Override
    protected void onCreate(Bundle savedInstanceState) {
        super.onCreate(savedInstanceState);
        setContentView(R.layout.activity_main);
}

    @Override
    public boolean onCreateOptionsMenu(Menu menu) {
        // Inflate the menu; this adds items to the action bar
        getMenuInflater().inflate(R.menu.menu_main, menu);
        return true;
    }

    @Override
    public boolean onOptionsItemSelected(MenuItem item) {
        // Handle action bar item clicks here. The action bar will
        // automatically handle clicks on the Home/Up button.
        // if you specify a parent activity in AndroidManifest.xml.
        int id = item.getItemId();
        //noinspection SimplifiableIfStatement
        if (id == R.id.action_settings) {
            return true;
        }
        return super.onOptionsItemSelected(item);
    }
}
```

You will be relieved to know that there is no need to understand any of this code. We are just going to use it to demonstrate the process of creating and testing an app in Android Studio.

Compiling and Running the App

So what we have now is actually a fully functioning app. It does not do much but it can be compiled and executed on our Android device. We can do this by tapping the Run button at the top of the display. This is a right pointing green triangle as shown in Figure 6.

This will compile the source code into an apk app file and run it either on an emulator or on an external phone or tablet device connected to your computer. Normally you will be given a choice between the emulator, which is called an Android Virtual Device, or AVD, and the real device that is connected to the PC. This is on a popup window as shown in Figure 7.

Figure 7. Choosing how to test the app.

If the dialog window does not appear you can click on the Run menu option at the top of the screen then select Edit configuration. This will open another dialog window that lets you force the IDE to always let you choose its Target.

Choosing an AVD

This is not the recommended choice for beginner programmers. It is much slower than developing on real devices. However, it must be included for completeness and because Google may improve the software at some stage in which case it would become a viable option. In any case, you should try it.

In this example, the default AVD offered is a Nexus 5 x86 device. You may prefer some other device, or the Nexus 5 emulator may not actually work on your computer. In fact the x86 devices have accelerators built-in to make them display more quickly and these do not always work properly.

In either case, you can install and use another emulator. You do this by opening the Tools option in the menu bar at the top of the screen. From this you select Android then AVD Manager and this opens a screen that shows the currently available AVDs which will only be the Nexus 5.

Clicking the Create Virtual Device button at the bottom left of the screen opens up the next dialog window where you can select a form factor, such as a tablet, then any one of a range of tablet devices. If you had trouble with the x86 device you should of course choose another one, such as an arm device. For example, if this is a Nexus 7 (2012) tablet the resulting AVD list will be as shown in Figure 8.

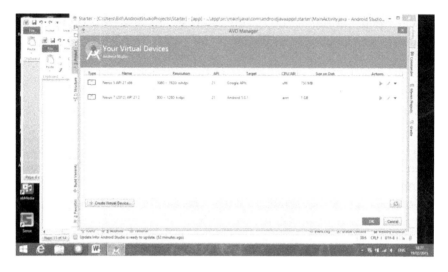

Figure 8. The list of selected AVDs.

You can delete the original by selecting it and using the delete key if you do not want to keep it as an option. Then you can close the dialog window and try the Run button again. This time you can select an AVD from the drop down box.

One point to note is that Android Studio is not very quick. It may take tens of seconds for the run dialog window to appear, especially the first time you try it when it has to build the app from scratch. This lethargy is typical of all IDEs that simulate an Android system on a Windows or other system, although you might find Eclipse slightly quicker. So you may have to be patient.

When you click the OK button the IDE will run the emulator and display your running app in it. However, again, you have to be patient since this can take several minutes and, even then, behave unreliably.

So while you are encouraged to try using the AVD, you might find yourself preferring to use a real device, which is much quicker. In fact, you should really test your apps on a range of real devices anyway.

Running on a Real Device

To use a real Android device you have to connect it to a USB socket on your computer. Then when you run your app you select the top option to choose a running device. However, if this is the first time you have run your own app on your phone or tablet then it will probably fail with a warning that the device is set to block installation of apps obtained from unknown sources. You are offered the choice of Cancel or Settings. Tap Settings to go to your device settings then find the Unknown Sources option and tap the checkbox to select it. You will be given a warning that this may be harmful to your device. Ignore this and tap OK. It is not malicious software since you have just written it. Now click Install. The app will be installed in your device and run.

So now you have created your own Android app and it is running on your phone or tablet.

The Unknown Sources option will remain enabled until you change it so if you want to run any more apps that do not come from the Play Store you can leave it set. If not you may want to cancel the setting.

When you run the app it should look like Figure 9. This is as it looks on a high resolution tablet device. It has a title bar at the top showing the app title, Starter and at the top of the screen it displays the text "Hello world".

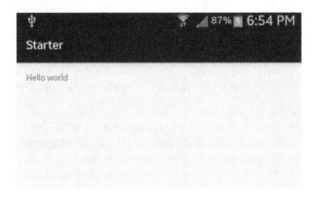

Figure 9. The Starter app running on a tablet device.

Also a new Starter icon will appear on the app screen of your device as shown in Figure 10.

Figure 10. The starter app icon.

You can tap this at any time to run the app like any other app in your device. It will be the default Android icon in the form of a green Android figure but we can change that later to our own design.

If you are wondering where the text came from, it came from the other files which were also created by Android Studio. These created a resource called R.layout.main which defines the user layout. This is used in the Java line

setContentView(R.layout.activity_main);

It refers to the default layout which is defined in the activity_main.xml file. This is found in the Starter/app/main/res/layout folder. This, in turn uses a text string defined in the Starter/app/main/res/values/string.xml file. And this has a line containing the text Hello world. If you feel like a little adventure you can try changing this.

However, this digression is just to let you see that there are other files in the app package. We are not going to use this layout file or the strings.xml file for the time being. All of our work will be in Java, so we will be changing the above Java statement in all of our apps to display our own Java user interface.

The App

So now we have already developed an app and it can be run in our Android device. It does not do very much but it is a real app. We can run it at any time by tapping the icon. What we can't do is submit it to the Google Play Store since it is not a final release version. We still have some work to do to create a release version and we will cover the process in the last chapter of the book.

However, we can copy this version to other devices and even distribute it to our friends and family if they are interested.

To do this we use the file system of the device to find the app file. It is called app-debug.apk and it will be in the folder, with the full name

Starter\app\build\outputs\apk\app-debug.apk

All you have to do is to copy this file to the other device. You can do this by USB connection, by sending it as an email attachment or through a cloud store such as Google Drive or Dropbox.

There is just one minor obstruction to overcome in the receiving device. It will probably not be set up to accept apps from unknown sources. So you will have to find this option and set it to accept. The process is the same one that you negotiated when you ran the app in your own device.

So app-debug.apk is your app. In fact it is the name of each app you develop. However, the displayed name is the app name, Starter. If you tap it in your device file list it will install itself and thereafter by executable from the icon. It is a debugging version rather than the final one but it runs exactly the same.

Using Android Studio

When you run Android Studio it will either open with the most recent project you were working on or it will open the welcome screen with a list of projects on the left, from which you can select one or you can create a new one.

If you are already working on a project and want to open another one the easiest way is to select File, Reopen which will present a list of your recent projects from which you can select one to open. If the project you want is not on the list, then you can select File, Open, then navigate to the project you want. Either process will probably offer you the option to open in a new window or to use the current window, replacing the existing project.

To close a project select File, Close Project, which will close the whole window. This does not delete the project from the project folder so you can reopen it again later. If it is the only open project then on the way out it may offer the welcome page again and if you also want to completely delete the project then select it and use the keyboard delete key. You can also delete a project from inside the IDE by right clicking on the project name and selecting the Delete option.

Otherwise the best way to completely delete a project from your computer is to navigate to its folder in the file system and use the delete key to remove it.

It is worth remembering that if you are experimenting with Studio and create some projects that you do not want to keep you can simply remove them by deleting the folders from the computer file system. Then they can be replaced by projects of the same name.

You can create a new project from the welcome screen or from the project window by selecting File, New Project, then going through the usual series of input windows to choose a name and domain, then a form factor, for which we will always use the phone and tablet with a Froyo minimum SDK, then the activity, for which we will always choose the basic Blank Activity, and finally you are asked for an Activity Name, for which we will always use the default, MainActivity.

Android Studio is not very well designed for beginner programmers so its selection of Activity templates is too advanced for our purposes. If we select the first one, to Add No Activity we get a blank project and have to add our own files including xml files. If we select the Blank Activity we get all the files created for us, including a MainActivity.java file with too much code. In this book we will go for the latter option and delete the superfluous code.

What Next

That is all you need to know about the IDE for now. You will get to know it quite well in the app developments that follow. All of them will use the same procedure that has been described here so you may want to refresh your memory on occasions. Each app will produce a version that can be used and distributed but not to the Google Play Store. That process will be covered in the last chapter.

However, now is a good time to practice using the IDE so if you have not been working along with the narrative, you should try to go through the entire process of developing the Starter app.

Remember if you want to find out more about the IDE you can open the Help, Help Topics menu and browse through that.

3. Java

The Aim

The aim is to produce an app that will draw a simple graphic shape on the screen and use it to introduce the basic theory of the Java language as used in Android systems. So this is where we finally start programming.

The output we hope to get is illustrated in Figure 1 for a smartphone.

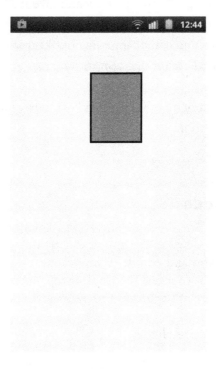

Figure 1. The Shape app running on an Android phone.

The Android Framework

An Android app at its very simplest level is an Activity and a View. Together these define the structure of an app.

The Activity is our Java program that drives the app and the View is the user interface. In general, Views can be written in XML in the form of Layouts but in this book we will define the View entirely in Java to keep it simple.

An Activity and a View are supplied as basic components in the Android API and all we have to do is customize them for our own apps. We will write our own activity and give it a specific name. In this and all the other apps in the book we will name the main activity as MainActivity. You can change this but keeping it constant makes it easier to copy code from one app to the next.

We will do the same for the view and call our version ShapeView throughout the book.

The Start Code

You can start to develop the app in exactly the same way as you did for the Starter app and end the same way too with an app in your Android emulator or a real device. But this time you will create a new app with the name, Shape, and the package name will be

com.androidjavaapps.shape

And, of course, you should change the com.androidjavaapps to your own domain name if you intend to distribute the app.

The IDE then generates the starter code for the new app. If we are working in Android Studio it opens with a Blank Activity and displays a couple of files in the workspace. Again we can remove all but the MainActivity.java file since we are working only in Java.

As usual, the initial build may be very slow. You should know something is happening by the Gradle messages and the progress indicator at the bottom of the window.

Then looking at the MainActivity.java file we can see that it is far from being blank. In fact there is quite a lot of code generated by Studio. In the Starter app we used this to demonstrate the development process but now we have to replace it with our own program.

We could have used the Add No Activity template when we created the app but this requires us to write all the xml files too, so we will start all our apps from the Blank Activity template and replace the Java code.

Our normal procedure for developing each app will be to copy and paste the code from the previous project window into the new one then make any required modifications and additions. This incremental way of developing is quite standard practice. It means the errors are always confined to the new parts and are more easily corrected. It also reduces the amount of coding required for each app so we will use this approach for all the apps.

So in this first case we have to delete all the Java code generated by Studio and type in our new code. Or, of course, you can just delete the unwanted code and change the ActionBarActivity to Activity. In either case you should end up with,

```
package com.androidjavaapps.shape;

import android.os.*;
import android.app.*;

public class MainActivity extends Activity {

    @Override
    protected void onCreate(Bundle savedInstanceState) {
        super.onCreate(savedInstanceState);
        setContentView(R.layout.activity_main);
    }
}
```

If typing errors are made they should be highlighted in red by the IDE and can be corrected. When there are no errors we can run the program by clicking on the triangular green run button. This program should produce the same output as the Starter app, with two differences. There will be no app name in the title bar at the top of the screen (since we have removed the ActionBarActivity) and the name change to Shape in the app icon. In fact, most published apps do not display the name in the title bar so this layout is quite common. And, in our later apps we will remove the title bar entirely.

Writing the New App

Now we have to make some changes and add some new code to start building our Shape app. At any time, we can run the program and test it. It will always replace the existing app with the new version.

The first thing to do is to edit the setContentView line to replace the default user interface with our own version. Then we need to add more lines to make our first Shape app. In doing this, remember Java is a very precise language and is case sensitive so even minor spelling errors will not be accepted.

However, if you do have some typos, the IDE will provide error warnings and underscore the offending code so you will get the chance to correct them. We will also try to make life easy by setting out the code as clearly as we can with indentation and blank spaces where appropriate.

So have a look at this and we will then discuss it.

The Program Code

Here is our first program. This is the source code we will enter into the IDE workspace to replace the content of MainActivity.java. You can rename it to something else if you want, such as MyActivity.java but there is not much to be gained from this so we will use the same name throughout the book.

```
package com.androidjavaapps.shape;

import android.os.*;
import android.app.*;
import android.view.*;
import android.content.*;
import android.graphics.*;

public class MainActivity extends Activity {

    ShapeView shapeView;

    public void onCreate(Bundle savedInstanceState) {
        super.onCreate(savedInstanceState);
        shapeView=new ShapeView(this);
        setContentView(shapeView);
    }

    public class ShapeView extends View{
        Paint paint= new Paint();
```

```
    public ShapeView(Context context){
       super(context);
    }

    public void onDraw(Canvas canvas){
       float width=8;
       float x=200,y=100, a=120, b=160;
       this.setBackgroundColor(Color.YELLOW);
       paint.setStrokeWidth(width);
       paint.setColor(Color.BLACK);
       paint.setStyle(Paint.Style.STROKE);
       canvas.drawRect(x, y, x+a,y+b, paint);
       paint.setColor(Color.RED);
       paint.setStyle(Paint.Style.FILL);
       canvas.drawRect(x, y, x+a,y+b, paint);
    }
  }
}
```

The Syntax

A program is a series of instructions to the computer or, to be more exact, its operating system. In Java these instructions are called statements and every line in the Shape program that ends with a semicolon is a statement. The other lines simply manage the statements by arranging them into blocks of statements contained between braces, { and }. These are sometimes described as compound statements. When the program is run, the blocks are executed, or run, in some programmed sequence but the statements within them are executed exactly in the order in which they are written.

There are three different types of brackets used in Java. There are curved brackets, or parentheses, (and) then there are square brackets, [and] and there are the curly brackets, or braces, { and }.

But, getting back to the story, before the program can be run as an app, this source code has to be translated from the programmer-friendly Java language to a format that can be understood by the Android operating system. So it has to be compiled by the IDE.

The Java language consists of the following components:-

- vocabulary, Java words sometimes described as keywords,
- grammar, which determines how the program is structured,
- punctuation, which includes the semicolons and the braces
- operators, which are shorthand symbols that replace words

This is the syntax of the language and in many respects it is like the syntax of a spoken language. However, the syntax of a programming language is much more precise. The words must be spelled correctly, the grammar used properly, the punctuation always included, the operators chosen appropriately and upper or lower case used exactly as required. On the other hand, the good news is that the vocabulary is much smaller than that of a spoken language so this part, at least, is easier to learn.

The last of these requirements refers to the fact that Java is case sensitive. A word such as package is not the same as Package or PACKAGE. So you have to be careful how you write and spell Java words. In fact, all of the words in the Java language are written entirely in lower case characters. The words you see in the Shape program that have upper case characters are data names, not Java words but Java does recognize these capitals.

On the other hand Java is not sensitive to white space, such as blank spaces and tabs, so we can layout the source code by inserting blank lines and indentation to make it as readable as possible. Of course, this does not apply to blank spaces in the middle of words. For example, pack age would not be recognized as package. Blank characters are used to separate words.

The Shape program starts with a single statement beginning with the word package then it has a short list of statements each beginning with the word import. All of these statements use dots to separate parts of the information included and this dot notation is an important feature of Java punctuation which you can see throughout the Shape program.

An import statement such as

import android.os.Bundle;

imports a specific component called Bundle with the path name android.os. In our code we will use statements like

import android.os.*;

The * symbol means everything, that is, import all the components in the path android.os.

So in these import statements we have used asterisks. These are to make our life easier (but our apps bigger) by importing all the components in each package instead of just the Bundle and Activity that we actually need. We will adopt this strategy throughout the book to make the coding as simple as possible.

Then follows a more complicated structure starting with the line

public class MainActivity extends Activity {

This is not a statement but it defines the beginning of a block of code that contains statements. In fact, the whole program is contained between this line and the last line of code, which just has a single closing brace, }. So our program is contained between a pair of braces - an opening brace, {, at the end of this line and a closing brace the other at the end of the code. You may see Java code written with the opening brace in the next line but it is more popular to place it at the end of the line and this is the style we will always use here. Remember we can layout our code any way we want to make it readable.

Within the program code there are some smaller blocks of code, each contained in its own pair of braces. We say they are nested within the outer block. You should be able to find four of these blocks. In each case the closing brace is lined up with the opening line and the other lines are indented to make the code readable and help you to pair up the braces. It can get very complicated with all these braces so every little helps.

Inside the blocks are the statements that make up the program. Each statement ends with a semicolon and may contain specific Java keywords, such as package and import. These are just words of the Java language and are always written in lower case characters. However, the data names must be written with the correct case, for example, MainActivity and Activity.

Statements

The statements are the basic ingredients of a program. They always involve processing data in some way so each statement is an instruction to perform some action on some data.

For example, in the first statement in the Shape program, the Java word, package, instructs Android to give the program a package name and the data that follows, com.androidjavaapps.shape, is the full name of the package. Then the statements beginning with the import keyword instruct Android to import pieces of specified code.

Further down the program there are different types of statement such as,

```
float width=8;
float x=200, y=100, a=120, b=160;
```

These tell Android to create names that will refer to particular data values. For example, width is associated with a value of 8. These are called assignment statements and the names are described as variable names. The same statements also include operators, in the form of the = symbols, the keyword, float, and punctuation in the form of the semicolons and commas.

Variables

The word float used in the above assignment statements is a Java keyword so it is always written in lower case letters. This word describes a type of data that is to be represented by a variable, in this case called width. The statement also instructs Android to give it the value 8, at least to begin with. The second statement declares four float type variables and gives them all starting values. We use commas to separate these pairs of names and values as an essential part of the Java syntax. Miss them out and the program will fail to compile.

The variable type, float, represents a floating point decimal number and tells Android to make enough storage space for its value. It is described as a simple data type or a primitive type. There are several other primitive types of which we will mention only five. These are

int   an integer number
float   a floating point decimal number
double   a double precision, high accuracy decimal number
boolean   a logical value of true or false
char   a single alphanumeric character

Variables are called variables because their values may change during the execution of a program, that is, at runtime. They are used to represent data values that are not known when the program is written and will probably not be known until they are calculated by the program or entered by the user. They are like the variables used in a mathematical formula.

Variable names are usually written in camel case. They start with lower case characters and if necessary add further parts each starting with an upper case letter. So we might have a float called lineThickness or an int called sizeOfScreen. This is not a compulsory style. It is only a convention, but a popular one and one that we will follow throughout the book.

In a Java program, all variables must be declared before they are used. Otherwise the program will try to process a variable that does not exist and it will crash. They can also be initialized to some starting value, again to avoid the program doing something silly.

And one last issue about variables is that it is frequently necessary to change a value from one type to another. For example a particular calculation may deliver an int instead of an expected float. Java will try to take care of the conversion, which is called casting. In fact Java will automatically cast any variable type to a more complex one simply by extending its memory allocation.

However the opposite cast from a more complex variable to a less complex one has to be specified by the programmer since we are forcing it into a smaller storage space and truncating its value. To do this we simply state the new type in brackets so to cast from a float xPosition to an int required by width we might have something like

width = (int) xPosition;

But xPosition = width would be OK.

Operators

Something else that turns up in many of the program statements is an operator. For example the = symbol used in the assignment statements is an assignment operator. It is not the same as the mathematical = sign which means "is equal to". This operator means "assign the value on the right to the variable on the left" We have another symbol for "is equal to" which is the double character ==.

There are many other operators in Java but we will not be using them until later. However, to get an idea of what an operator is, here are some arithmetic operators

+ the plus operator to add a number
- the minus operator to subtract a number
* the times operator to multiply by a number
/ the divide operator to divide by a number
( ) brackets are used to hold expressions to be evaluated first

And a few comparison operators

== is equal to
> is greater than
< is less than
!=is not equal to

Bill Tait

4. Objects

The Package

The Shape app is an object. Its full name is defined in the very first statement.

package com.androidjavaapps.shape;

This declares the package name of your app, in this case, com.androidjavaapps.shape, which you chose when you created the project. It is important that it is different from the full name of any other app on the Play Store or on someone's Android device. This is the name that is used to find and run the app. If it is not unique there will be problems. In fact, Google will not let you upload an app to the Play Store if it does not have a unique package name.

To get a unique package name we use our own domain name. Since only one registrant can own a particular domain name, this ensures that our package name is unique. We get the package name by writing the domain name backwards then adding the app name and converting it all to lower case. So if the domain name is androidjavaapps.com and the app name is Shape we get com.androidjavaapps.shape, as above.

We use dots to separate the components of a package name. This dot notation is an important part of the Java syntax and of all other object-oriented programming languages. It will become a familiar notation.

Another point that might need to be explained is that the app name is not the same as the package name but only a shortened version. There can be another app on the Play Store or your phone called Shape as long as it is in a different folder, that is, a different package. This is the same way the folders on your computer are organized except that here we use dots instead of backward or forward slashes to indicate subfolders.

The Imports

The next few statements in the Shape app are the import statements. These get you off to a quick start by copying reusable code components into your program. The components are called classes but this may not be very clear. What we actually need to import is

```
import android.os.Bundle;
import android.app.Activity;
import android.view.View;
import android.content.Context;
import android.graphics.Canvas;
import android.graphics.Paint;
import android.graphics.Color;
```

Each of these statements imports a class. The first imports the class called Bundle which is in the os subfolder of the android folder. So the dots represent subfolders like the backslashes used by Windows. It has the package name android.os.Bundle. This is the full name of the Bundle class, which we are going to use in our program. The other import statements copy Activity, View, Context, Canvas, Paint and Color classes into our program. A class is just a type of object and the order in which they are imported is not important.

However, some IDEs may not do this but instead use a * symbol instead of a class name. In computing, the * character usually means everything and here it is no different. The * indicates that all the classes in the package should be imported.

So we might have

```
import android.os.*;
import android.app.*;
import android.view.*;
import android.content.*;
import android.graphics.*;
```

This means fewer import lines need to be used but a slightly bigger program will be created since a number of unnecessary classes will be imported.

Classes and Objects

Java is an object-oriented programming language. It is not limited to its own primitive data types. It can use other data types defined outside the language. So a program can have many more data types than the built-in ones and they can be quite complex types, custom designed for the program. These are called classes.

When you write a new app you are inventing new classes and in effect writing your own version of Java. This is exactly what Android has done in its API.

We can use these classes in the same way as the primitives, that is, we create variables of the classes and assign names to them. However, in this case, the variables are said to represent objects rather than simple data. So an object is a realization, or an instance of a class.

Since the classes are not actually part of the Java language, their names are not restricted to lower case characters. In fact, to make this clear, they always start with upper case letters. They can be created by the programmer but a number of reusable classes are also provided by the Android system itself. This is sometimes described as an API, or Application Programming Interface. We will just refer to the collection of classes as Android.

There are two huge advantages of object-oriented programming. One is that we can work in a language with a very high level of abstraction

– one that uses concepts that are common in spoken English. For example we can make "ball" objects that can "move" about the screen and "bounce" off the sides. This is a big step up from floating point numbers and single characters. The other advantage is that these objects are reusable. We can write lots of ball apps using the same Ball class. This can save us a lot of development time and it also helps to make our apps more error free since reused objects are already tested.

And just another reminder on naming conventions – classes always start with upper case letters, but object names, since they are variables, always start with lower case letters.

Creating Objects

Creating a variable to represent an object is slightly different from creating a float or an int variable. This is because the class is a much more complex data type that requires more storage space. It also has an internal structure that will vary from one class to another. Classes need to have their own internal variables and ways of processing them. So we require a special way to create objects.

This involves the use of a keyword, new, and a special function called a constructor. An example in the above code is

    Paint paint= new Paint();

This declares a new object called paint, of the class Paint, and assigns it to a new object by using the function Paint(). This is the constructor that creates an object that we will use to paint our shape - like a combination of paintbrush and paint pot.

The constructor is defined in the class definition and constructs the object to some given formula. The Paint class has been imported into our app so its constructor is available for use in our program. The constructor always has the same name as the class, so it starts with an upper case letter.

You might also notice that we have used the same name for the class and its object with only one difference - the object name starts with a lower case letter and the class starts with a capital. This is enough to make them quite different names and it is a strategy we will use whenever we only want only one object of some class.

Creating a New Class

We can define a new class inside the definition of an existing class in which case it is called an inner class. The alternative is to define a class outside of any other classes and in its own file with the same name. An inner class has easy access to all the code of the containing class. An outer class is more independent of the containing class and therefore more reusable. We will use both approaches.

A new class is defined by declaring the class keyword and its name. We can also add access keywords, such as public or private to allow it to be used by other classes or not. And it can, and usually does, extend some other class. For example,

public class ShapeView extends View

Then the class code is written inside a pair of braces. This has three components,

- Attributes: These define the properties of objects of the class and are represented by a set of variables, which can represent primitive data types or other objects.

- Constructor: At least one function that defines how objects of the class are to be built.

- Methods: These are functions which define the behavior of objects of the class. A method is used by an object of the class to do something.

The ShapeView Class

In the Shape program we have defined a new inner class called ShapeView. It is inner because it is our only view class and we want it to see all the Activity attributes in later versions of the program. Its code is as follows:-

```
public class ShapeView extends View{

    public ShapeView(Context context){
        super(context);
    }

    public void onDraw(Canvas canvas){
        Paint paint= new Paint();
        float width=8;
        float x=200,y=100, a=120, b=160;
        this.setBackgroundColor(Color.YELLOW);
        paint.setStrokeWidth(thickness);
        paint.setColor(Color.BLACK);
        paint.setStyle(Paint.Style.STROKE);
        canvas.drawRect(x, y, x+a,y+b, paint);
        paint.setColor(Color.RED);
        paint.setStyle(Paint.Style.FILL);
        canvas.drawRect(x, y, x+a,y+b, paint);
    }
}
```

The word public just means that the class can be used by other classes outside this one. It has public accessibility. The opposite alternative is private, which means that it can only be used by the containing class. Sometimes there are reasons to keep our class contents isolated from the rest of our app but we will mostly use public access without thinking much about it for the time being.

Then we have the word, class, and the class name, ShapeView followed by another keyword, extends. This means that we do not have to write our class from scratch but instead we extend an existing class. In this case it is the View class which we just imported. This is how we reuse Android classes.

The ShapeView class inherits all the attributes, constructor and methods of the View class. It is sometimes described as a subclass of View, and View is described as a super class of ShapeView. Sometimes we may just refer to ShapeView as a View, since it is a kind of View.

The View class defines objects that are drawn on the screen but it has no actual form so it is normally extended to a class that does have a specific form. We can also use in it an xml file to build a user interface and although that is an aspect of Android development that you should eventually learn, we will not be using it here. In fact, our user interface will just be a blank screen on which a graphic shape can be drawn.

The next piece of code defines the constructor, ShapeView(Context context). This has only one statement,

super(context);

What is does is simply run the constructor of the super class View, without any further code. It also has a parameter declared inside the brackets, as

Context context

The Context class was also imported into our app and inside the brackets we need to declare a variable, context, to represent a Context object since the super class, View, needs to know the current context, which is essentially the activity that is to be used.

Methods

Methods are described as functions in other programming languages but in Java they always belong to classes and are described as methods. A method represents a short piece of code that describes some behavior of objects of the class. Each method has its own unique name within the class, but may have the same name as a method in another class. Conventionally, this starts with a lower case character and may be camel case, followed by a pair of curved brackets (or parentheses). These may contain data in the form of arguments that are to be processed by the method.

A method is called (or executed or run) anywhere in the program simply by stating its name and any data it may be asked to process. These are entered as arguments, in the form of variables or constant values, inside the brackets. For example,

setContentView(shapeView);

This statement causes the program to jump to the definition of the Activity method setContentView and execute it, using the arguments as input parameters. The method is, of course, inherited by our MainActivity class. So we are now looking at the ShapeView user interface on the device. Then it returns to the exact point in the code from which it was called and goes on to execute the next statement.

In general, a method may just do something, such as set the user interface, as above, or it may calculate and return a single value to the point where it was called where it may be used. In this case it acts like an expression. An example might be to get the current painting color and assign it to a variable, currentColor in

currentColor = paint.getColor();

When a method is defined it should indicate what type of variable it returns or be defined as void if it returns nothing. For example, our Shape app has an onDraw() method to draw a shape on the screen. This is declared as public and void. Public means it can be seen and used by code outside of the ShapeView class and void means that it does not return any value to the code that called it.

The method also declares a variable called canvas of the class Canvas inside the brackets. This means it expects to be given a copy of the current canvas object used by this view. However, onDraw() is not actually called by our program but by the operating system. Android decides when to refresh the screen by calling this method. It has to be called onDraw() so that Android can call it.

Dot Notation

Dots are used in object-oriented programming languages to indicate a subcomponent. In particular, a dot is used to describe an attribute or a method of a particular object. So in the Shape app we use

paint.setStrokeWidth(width);
paint.setColor(Color.*BLACK*);

to run the setStroke() then the setColor() methods of paint. The first call passes an argument which is the width of line and the second one passes an argument which is the color in which it is to be drawn.

If we do not know what the name of the object will be at runtime we can use the keyword, this, meaning the current object.

this.setBackgroundColor(Color.*YELLOW*);

On the other hand, if we know it is an object of the class containing the method we can just drop the object name completely. Android will always try the current class first So, setBackgroundColor() would also work in this case.

Scope

This discussion of dot notation is also related to the scope of a variable or method. The scope is that part of the application in which it is available for use. We often describe this as the code where it is "visible", or the code from which it can be "seen".

In general any variable declared in the class attributes is visible to all the methods in the class or any other inner classes defined in the class. It is described as an instance variable since it is a property of all instances, or objects, of the class. In other words a variable is downwardly visible. However, the reverse is not true. A variable declared in a method or an inner class is not visible to the containing class. It is described as a local variable as opposed to an instance variable.

For example, the shapeView object declared in MainActivity is visible to all methods of the activity which is our app.

Conversely, the width variable declared in the onDraw() method is not visible outside the method. In fact, when onDraw() is finished executing all its variables are deleted to save storage space.

A problem arises when we need to access a variable from one method of a class that is defined in another method of the same class. This would require sideways visibility which is not possible. When we need to have two or more methods accessing the same variables they have to be declared as instance variables. They don't have to be initialized there. That can be done anywhere and since it is the same variable, stored in the same memory location, any change in its value by one method is seen by all the other methods that use it.

An example of this practice is the declaration of our View object,

ShapeView shapeView;

This makes shapeView an instance variable that can be seen by all methods of the MainActivity class. However, it is only given a value in the onCreate() method

shapeView = new ShapeView(this);

This is a standard way of creating new objects.

And, incidentally the statement passes "this" object to the View constructor. This represents the current object which is an object of the MainActivity class.

The Program Class

The app itself is a new class, which we have called MainActivity. An object of this class is created by Android when the app is run. It is the only time we do not have to create our own object and the only time we do not know its name.

The main structure of the class is

```
public class MainActivity extends Activity {

    ShapeView shapeView;

    public void onCreate(Bundle savedInstanceState) {
        super.onCreate(savedInstanceState);
        shapeView=new ShapeView(this);
        setContentView(shapeView);
    }

    public class ShapeView extends View{
    }
}
```

The first line declares that the structure that follows is a class and that it is public. This means that it can be seen by other objects outside the class – such as the Android operating system.

Then it states the name of the class, MainActivity, and that it extends another class called Activity. The Activity class was imported into our app and the new MainActivity class copies all of its code and extends it. This means it adds more code to make it more specific to our aims. So MainActivity is an Activity with some additions.

Then the program code is contained between the opening and closing braces. It starts with a declaration of a ShapeView variable to represent an object of a ShapeView class. This is the only attribute of our program class and it is declared here but not initialized. Instead, it is initialized in the onCreate() method.

This strategy of splitting the declaration and the initialization is quite common. We need to declare it as a global attribute, or instance variable, so that it can be seen by all the methods of MainActivity. On the other hand it is better to give it a value in the onCreate() method which is run every time the app is restarted – which is quite often.

Also, we have to give the constructor an argument which represents the current activity. We don't know what the object name is so we use the keyword, this, to indicate the current object.

The onCreate() Method

There is only one method in our program class and it is the onCreate() method,

```
public void onCreate(Bundle savedInstanceState) {
    super.onCreate(savedInstanceState);
    shapeView=new ShapeView(this);
    setContentView(shapeView);
}
```

It is sometimes preceded by the keyword @Override. This is useful to remind the programmer that the method extends, or overrides an existing Activity method. It is also checked by the compiler which can pick up any override errors.

This method is what runs our app and sets up any initial data values. It starts with "on" because it is run "on" the program object being created by Android. Any method whose name starts with "on" is run by the operating system. Android determines the name of this method so we have no choice here.

Inside its brackets it has a single argument. This is

Bundle savedInstanceState.

It declares a local variable, savedInstanceState to represent an object of the Bundle class. We don't have to call it savedInstanceState but this is quite a common choice. It refers to the state of the program object (its instance) when the app was stopped. When the method is run by the Android system it collects anything held in this object. This is necessary if it has been running already and is restarted for some reason. Then any data it has been using can be picked up in the onCreate() method for continued use. Android apps frequently have to restart for example when the device is rotated from portrait to landscape mode or the reverse.

Then there is a statement that runs a method called

super.onCreate(savedInstanceState);

The keyword, super, represents the parent class from which the present one was extended and the dot links it to its version of onCreate() which it now runs. This way we pick up any basic code that we need in the new version. It uses the same argument, savedInstanceState.

Then the method sets the current view, that is, the screen display, to a new view. We have to give our variable, shapeView a value by initializing it to a new object of ShapeView then we use setContentView(shapeView); to finish the job and end with a closing brace so the whole method is contained in braces.

The onDraw() Method

The last part of our class is a the onDraw() method and it is the main process that takes place in our app. This is where the shape is drawn. This too is defined as a public method as required by the original definition in the API. Then it declares a return type of void, so it will return nothing.

The method has to be called onDraw(). We have no choice in the matter. This is the name of the function that is called by Android when it needs to refresh the display. Again, the "on" part means "on redrawing".

The first statement inside the class declares a variable called paint, to represent a Paint object. In this book we will follow the convention of using the same name for a single object of a class, in this case, paint and Paint. We could have use myPaint or something but paint is simpler. Also we have decided to declare the paint object inside onDraw() which means we will not be able to see it outside of this method. All of our drawing will be done inside onDraw().

```
public void onDraw(Canvas canvas){
    Paint paint = new Paint()
    float width=8;
    float x=200,y=100, a=120, b=160;
    this.setBackgroundColor(Color.YELLOW);
    paint.setStrokeWidth(width);
    paint.setColor(Color.BLACK);
    paint.setStyle(Paint.Style.STROKE);
    canvas.drawRect(x, y, x+a,y+b, paint);
    paint.setColor(Color.RED);
    paint.setStyle(Paint.Style.FILL);
    canvas.drawRect(x, y, x+a,y+b, paint);
}
```

The method needs a Canvas object to draw on. This is sent to it when the method is called from the View super class. Then we can use it in the onDraw() method. The canvas has drawing methods that allow the programmer to set out drawings that are then transferred to the device screen. It is called automatically by Android, usually many times per second when the screen is refreshed.

In this case, onDraw() needs a variable to represent the width of the lines to be drawn. This must be a float variable and we will call it width and give it a starting value of 8 pixels. Then we need some variables to represent the x and y coordinates of the position of our shape and its width, a, and height, b. We will make these floats too.

As a matter of interest, we could make them int variables. They are used as arguments in the canvas.drawRect() method which requires floats but it will change the ints to floats when it receives them. This is an example of casting and it is a way of changing the variable type. Sometimes it is not done automatically by the program and we have to do it explicitly, but not here.

In Java graphics, screen position is measured from the left edge of the screen to the left side of the shape and from the top of the screen down to the top of the shape. Normally this is the top left corner of the shape. In computer graphics the x and y positions on the screen are almost always measured in from the left and down from the top of the display – like text but not like mathematics.

So our shape will be 200 pixels in from the left and 100 pixels down from the top. It will be 120 pixels wide and 160 pixels high. A pixel, by the way, is a picture element of the display and in the example shown below for the Android phone there are 480 pixels across by 800 pixels vertically on the screen.

Now we set the background color of the view to yellow, with the statement

    this.setBackgroundColor(Color.YELLOW);

As usual, the keyword, this, refers to the current object, which is, in this case, shapeView. This is an object that inherits all the View class methods, one of which is setBackgroundColor() and takes as an argument a Color class constant, Color.YELLOW. And yes, YELLOW must be all upper case which is how we usually name class constants.

Now what we have to do is set the paint color and draw a graphic element. Each time we set the color or line width the value will remain in use until it is changed. So the following sets the line width with setStroke(width), then sets the color to black, then uses setStyle(Paint.Style.STROKE) to draw in a line style and draws it with the paint object on the canvas with

    canvas.drawRect(x, y, x+a, y+b, paint).

So this draws an outline rectangle at x and y of width a and height b, that is, to x+a and y+b, using the paint object.

Then we use setColor() again to set the paint color to RED, choose a paint fill style and draw another rectangle filled with red paint.

Running the App

Now we have finished our first app. If there are any errors showing these have to be found and corrected. We should find any errors underlined in red so they should be easy to find. When there are no more errors we can run the app in the emulator or the development device by tapping the Run icon at the top of the display. This is a right pointing green triangle. The process is the same as we used for the starter app in Chapter 2, in the section on Running the App

When you run the app it should look like Figure 1. This is as it looks on a high resolution tablet, on the left, and on a much smaller resolution phone screen, on the right. It appears much smaller on the higher resolution. This is because we fixed the positions and sizes.

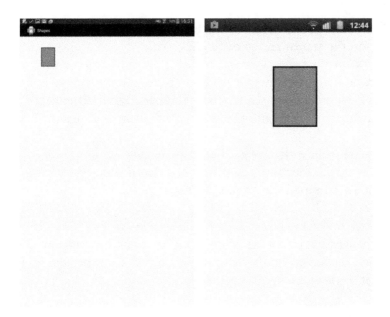

Figure 1. The Shape app on a tablet (left) and phone (right).

Also a new default Shape icon will have appeared on your app screen. You can tap this at any time to run the app like any other app in your device.

You may notice that the rectangle looks bigger in the small screen of a phone than in the larger screen of a tablet. This is because we gave it a fixed width and height so looks bigger in the small screen of the phone compared to the larger screen of the tablet. We would really like our apps to look the same in all screens. So we have to draw shape to scale.

This is something we will deal with in the next app.

Versions

Now it is your turn to experiment. You can start by copying all the Shape code into your own IDE and getting it to run on your Android device. Then you should try to change the app in some way. You might like to draw a different rectangle or more of them at different positions on the screen and in different colors.

Writing code is a great way to learn how to program but there is a problem. If you make too many errors you may find it difficult to recover the original code and you will have to write it all again.

Programmers frequently update their code to new versions but before they do so, they save the original so that if things go wrong they can always reopen the original and start again.

So, when we make a major change to our app we would like to keep a copy of the original in case anything goes wrong and we have to start again. The best way to do this is to make a copy of our project folder and save it somewhere in our computer.

All you have to do is navigate to the AndroidProjects folder on your computer. This should contain a Shape folder which contains your project files. We want to make a copy of this folder and save it somewhere else as a backup copy. If you need it later you can just copy and paste the backup back into the project folder.

The original version of Shape can now be modified without fear of losing the work you have already done. You can experiment with the original version to see what changes you can make.

Bill Tait

5. Graphics

The Aim

The aim of this chapter is to introduce all the graphics methods that we will use in the rest of the book. We will do this by developing a new app called Graphic. In addition we will introduce methods for producing a much wider range of colors. And finally we will put our graphics code for drawing a figure where it belongs – in its own separate class.

Graphics Methods

Android graphics uses a Paint object to draw on a Canvas object within a View context. Both the Paint and Canvas classes provide methods for drawing. We have already met three paint methods. For example, if paint is the name of a Paint object then we have

- paint.setStrokeWidth(width)   where width is described by a float variable as a number of pixels. This sets the width of the next lines to be drawn.

- paint.setColor(color) where color is an int variable representing the color value, such as Color.RED. This is a constant defined in the Color class which is actually an integer. Class constants are always written all in upper case to make it clear they are constants rather than variables.

- paint.setStyle(style) where style is Paint.Style.STROKE or FILL. Note that Paint is a class name as is Stroke.

Also we used a Canvas method to draw a rectangle. For a canvas object of the Canvas class this would be

- canvas.drawRect(x1, y1, x2, y2, paint) where x1,y1 are the coordinates of the top left corner of the rectangle and x2,y2 are the coordinates of the bottom right corner and paint is an object of the Paint class.

We also have a View method, inherited by ShapeView, to set the background color, view.setBackgroundColor(color) where color again represents an int color value. Here, view, refers to a View object, such as shapeView. However, the method is usually called inside the view object itself so we can use this.setBackgroundColor(color) or just setBackgroundColor(color).

Now we will add a few more graphics methods,

- canvas.drawCircle(x, y, r, paint). This draws a circle centered on the point x, y and radius r.

- canvas.drawLine(x1, y1, x2, y2, paint). This draws a line from x1, y1 to x2, y2 using the current value of paint.

Then there is the Path class. It has a constructor Path(), which just creates a new path object, and has a large number of methods. If path is the Path object these include

- path.moveTo(x, y) moves the path pointer to the position given by the float values x and y.

- path.lineTo(x, y) draws a line to the point defined by the float values x and y.

- path.close() completes the closed path by joining the last point drawn to the first one.

- path.reset() clears the path and allows the variable to be reused to draw another path.

- canvas.drawPath(path, paint) finally draw the path that has been defined by path using the current values of paint.

There are lots more but these are enough to draw some quite complex shapes. We simply draw these basic shapes on top of each other on the same canvas object.

Color

There are several ways to define a color in Java. So far we have been using colors defined in the Color class, such as Color.RED and Color.YELLOW, to represent colors. These are very easy to use but they have a limited range. We can only have BLACK, BLUE, CYAN, DKGRAY, GRAY, GREEN, LTGRAY, MAGENTA, RED, TRANSPARENT, WHITE or YELLOW.

They are also quite unusual in two respects. First they are constants rather than variables so they named with all upper case letters. The value of Color.RED cannot change. Secondly, they are class data values rather than object values. There can be no objects of the Color class because there is only one set of colors. For example, a yellow color object would be the same as any other yellow color object. So they are class constants written with the class name and a capitalized value.

There is another way to define colors that gives us a lot more choice but is more difficult to use. This is based on the idea that any color can be constructed from a combination of red, green and blue components. We assign one byte of computer memory to each component. One byte is an 8 bit number that can have 256 different values from 0 to 255. Then we use three of these as a three byte integer number of which the left byte, that is the highest part of the number, is the red component, the next byte is the green component and the last byte is the blue component.

This gives us 16,777,216 colors. For example, we could specify a color by the integer 16,000,000. This is a very high number so it is some shade of red. Similarly, 65,000 would be a shade of green and 250 would be a bright blue. And 16,065,250 would be a mixture of these components.

However, there is an easier and more precise way to use these numbers and that is to specify the three components as separate numbers from 0 to 255. Then 255, 0, 0 is the brightest red, 0, 255, 0 is the brightest green and 0, 0, 255 is the brightest blue. We might also have 255, 255, 255 which is white, 0, 0, 0 which is black and 100, 100, 100 which is gray. Some other examples are, 200, 200, 0 which is yellow, 200, 50, 0 which is orange, and 0, 100, 250 which is greenish blue.

The Color class provides methods that combine these components to make a complete color. It can also add a fourth component to specify the opaqueness or alpha component of the color. An alpha of 0 is totally transparent and a value of 255 is totally opaque with other values giving various degrees of partial transparency in between these extremes.

The methods are again class methods and are

Color.rgb(int red, int green, int blue)   and
Color.argb(int alpha, int red, int green, int blue)

They can be used in Paint methods, for example,

paint,setColor(Color. rgb(int red, int green, int blue))   and
paint.setColor(Color.argb(int alpha, int red, int green, int blue))

So here we are using a Paint method to run a Color class method to set the painting color. The Color method returns a color value which is then use as the argument in paint.setColor().

In passing, you might like to note that these components are sometimes expressed as hexadecimal numbers, such as ff0000, 00ff00 and 0000ff, but we will stick to decimals throughout the book.

Gradient

We can also add color gradients to our shapes sometimes to give the impression of three dimensions. The most common gradients are linear gradients and radial gradients. They are defined by two classes, LinearGradient and RadialGradient. To use gradients we first have to create objects of these classes with all the data required to define the gradients then we use a paint method to set the gradient.

We can create a gradient object from these classes in the usual way. A linear gradient is created with,

- LinearGradient linearGradient
  = new LinearGradient(float x1, float y1, float x2, float y2, int c1, int c2, Shader.TileMode.mode)

This creates a gradient that changes along a straight line from the point x1, y1 to the point x2, y2. The starting color, at x1, y1 is c1 and the end color is c2. It will draw a series of lines across this path this fill the figure. It is illustrated in Figure 2 for a gradient from the top of a rectangle to the bottom where in this case the gradient starts and stops at the rectangle boundaries. We could draw the gradient path diagonally and we could start and terminate it inside or outside the rectangle.

The last parameter, Shader.TileMode.mode can have one of three values for mode, namely, CLAMP, MIRROR or REPEAT. The CLAMP constant ends the gradient and extends the final color if the gradient ends inside a shape. The MIRROR constant repeats the gradient as a mirror image, that is, in reverse. The REPEAT constant repeats the pattern. An example of the CLAMP is

LinearGradient linearGradient
= new LinearGradient(x1,y1,x2,y2, c1, c2,Shader.TileMode.*CLAMP*);

A radial gradient is also illustrated in Figure 2. This is declared and initialized in the same way as the linear gradient but requires different parameters. These are x and y the coordinates of the center of the gradient circle, radius, its radius and again, c1, c2 the start and end colors and the mode constant.

- RadialGradient radialGradient =
  new RadialGradient(float x, float y, float radius, int c1, int c2, Shader.TileMode.mode)

Again x and y are the center point of the gradient and may not be the same as the center point of the shape that it fills. CLAMP will stop changing the color if the gradient terminates inside the shape, MIRROR will reverse the gradient and REPEAT will repeat it until the shape is filled.

In Figure 2 the center of the gradient is half a radius up and to the left of the center of the shape to produce a three dimensional highlighted effect with light coming from the top left direction. It is produced with code of the form

RadialGradient radialGradient =
new RadialGradient(x-r/2, y-r/2, 3*r/2, c1, c2,
Shader.TileMode.CLAMP);

In this example, r is the radius of a circular figure being painted. The gradientstarts at x-r/2, and y-r/2 and extends for a gradient radius of 3/r/2 to make sure it covers the whole shape.

Then we use the paint methods instead of the style and color methods,

paint.setShader(linearGradient)   or
paint.setShader(radialGradient)

Figure 2. A linear gradient and a radial gradient

The difference between a ball image without and with a gradient is illustrated in Figure 3.

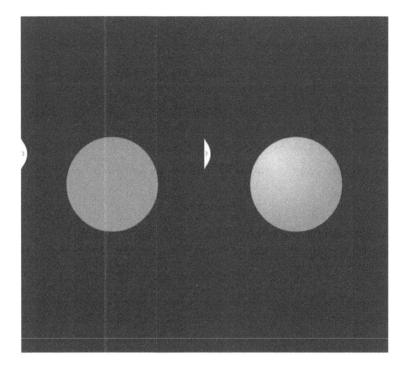

Figure 3. A ball shape without and with a color gradient.

A Graphic App

We will create a new app called Graphic in the usual way. Then we will copy all the code from Shape into Graphic as our starting code. All we have to do is to change the app name to graphic in the package name

package com.androidjavaapps.graphic;

So far we have been programming the onDraw() method of ShapeView to draw shapes. Now we want to move on to more complex figures so we really need to separate the drawing code from the rest of the program. Then we can edit it easily without having to alter the ShapeView code and we can easily replace any figure with a different one.

For this we need to create a new class that will contain all the code for the drawing. Then we can revise it or replace it easily and reuse it in later apps. We can even build up a library of figures from which we can copy and paste code into any particular app. In this case, we will call it Figure.

To accommodate the new class we have to make some modifications to the ShapeView code and remove the drawing code from ShapeView's onDraw() to relocate it in a separate Figure class.

So the modified app class is

```
package com.androidjavaapps.graphic;

import android.os.*;
import android.app.*;
import android.view.*;
import android.content.*;
import android.graphics.*;

public class MainActivity extends Activity {

    ShapeView shapeView;

    @Override
    protected void onCreate(Bundle savedInstanceState) {
        super.onCreate(savedInstanceState);
        shapeView=new ShapeView(this);
        setContentView(shapeView);
    }
```

```
public class ShapeView extends View{
    Figure figure;

    public ShapeView(Context context){
        super(context);
        float size=200;
        float x=200;
        float y=200;
        int c=Color.rgb(180,80,40);      // orange color
        int ch=Color.rgb(200,200,200);   // light highlight
        int background=Color.rgb(40, 50, 60);  // grey blue
        setBackgroundColor(background);
        figure=new Figure(size,x,y,c,ch);   // constructor
    }

    public void onDraw(Canvas canvas){
        figure.draw(canvas);
    }
}
```

Here, the new Figure object is declared in the instance variables and initialized in the ShapeView constructor. It can be used with any Figure class whose constructor is set up to expect five arguments, size, x, y, c and ch. These define the size, position and two main colors of the figure so they should be quite easily reused.

Then the onDraw() method simply calls the draw() method of the Figure class and passes it a copy of the canvas object. This ensures that the Figure will draw on the same canvas that has been created by ShapeView.

You might also note that the creation of a new paint object has been removed since this will now be done in the Figure class. It means that any drawing we do must be in the Figure class.

The Figure Class

To make it fully reusable, we will create the new Figure class outside of the activity and add it to the project. To create a new class in Android Studio, you must find the java folder in the project window. This usually means opening up the app folder, then src, and main and selecting the project folder, com.androidjavaapps.graphic.

Then if you select File, New you are offered a selection of new items that you can create, of which the first is a Java Class. On selecting that, you get a new window into which you enter the name of the new class, as illustrated in Figure 4. Now the new Figure.java file is listed in the java folder and probably opened in the workspace ready for editing.

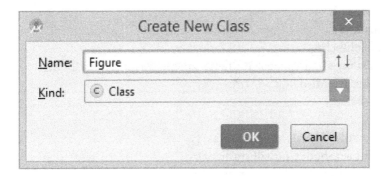

Figure 4. The Create New Class window.

It will probably have some initial code, such as

package com.androidjavaapps.graphic;

public class MainActivity {
}

This should be replaced by the Figure class code below designed to draw a ball object on the screen,

85

```
package com.androidjavaapps.graphic;

import android.graphics.*;

public class Figure {
    float size, x, y;
    float r;      // radiius of ball
    int c, ch;
    RadialGradient radialGradient;
    Paint paint =new Paint();

    public Figure(float size, float x, float y, int c, int ch){
        this.size=size;
        this.x=x;
        this.y=y;
        r=size/2;
        this.c=c;
        this.ch=ch;
        radialGradient = new RadialGradient(x-r/2,y-r/2,r*3/2,
ch,c,Shader.TileMode.CLAMP);
    }

    public void draw(Canvas canvas){
        paint.setShader(radialGradient);
        canvas.drawCircle(x, y, r, paint);
    }
}
```

This is a little complicated because we have to deal with a scope problem. The figure parameters are passed to the constructor, which is the only way to get them into Figure, but they are then used in the draw() method which is out of scope. The only way to make them visible to draw() is to use Figure class attributes, in this case with the same names, and assign the values of the parameters to these variables. Now draw() can use the variables, size, x, y, c and ch.

So we have a long list of instance variables and a rather tedious list of assignments in the constructor, such as this.size = size. Here the the, this, keyword refers, of course, to the instance variable and is assigned to the value of size transferred in the constructor parameters from ShapeView. The same is true for all the other attribute variables.

We also add another variable, r, to represent the radius of the ball figure we are drawing in this version of Figure. This is completely local to the Figure class since we have no need to use it outside. We also need a RadialGradient for this figure and its own new Paint object. These are all declared as Figure instance variables then initialized in the constructor.

The draw() method has only one parameter, a Canvas object. This is sent from ShapeView so it is the same canvas that is used in the ShapeView onDraw() method to draw on the device screen. We now use this canvas to draw a circle with the ball gradient.

When the app is run, a ball object is displayed in the top left corner of the screen as illustrated in Figure 5. The size of the ball is fixed so it will look smaller on large screen than on small ones.

Figure 5. The ball figure with a radial gradient

So now you should try your hand at producing your own version of this app. You can use different ball parameters and draw more than one ball.

6. Drawing

The Aim

The aim now is to draw a more complicated shape using the graphics Path class and the color methods. So we will write a new version of the Figure class. At the same time we will try to improve the display to make it look more like a finished product. So we will extend the Graphic app in a number of ways,

- First we will remove the title bar so that the app displays on a clear screen.
- Then we will try to scale and position the drawing to match the size of the screen on our device so that it will look the same on all Android devices, whatever their screen sizes.
- Then, we will deal with the problem of reorientation. You may have noticed in the previous apps that when the user rotates the device from portrait mode to landscape mode, or vice versa, the size and position of the figure changes. This is because reorientation causes the app to stop and restart. This happens on all devices and in all apps that are not specifically programmed not to do so. So it is something we will have to start looking at.

- Draw a different figure, this time of a car, to practice using the Path class and its methods and to experience the advantages of having a reusable Figure class.

The outcome we are looking for is as illustrated in Figures 1 and 2.

Figure 1. The Drawing app in portrait mode.

Figure 2. The Drawing app in landscape mode.

First, though, we need some more Java theory in the form of Decisions.

Java Decisions

A decision is a point in a program where the value of some variable or expression is tested and the program takes one of two or more alternative paths depending on the result of the comparison. It is also called a branch or a selection.

A decision is based on the use of the comparison operators mentioned in Chapter 3. They include

== is equal to
> is greater than
< is less than
!= is not equal to

For example, we might have an expression x > y. This may evaluate to true or false. It is true if the value of x is currently greater than y, otherwise it is false. We could even assign it to a Boolean variable moreThan with

moreThan = x>y

If x=5 and y=3 the expression is true. If x=3 and y=5 it is false. But what if x=4 and y=4? Then of course, it is false since x is not greater than y but only equal to it.

We can use a decision to execute some code by using a Java, if, statement. This is a compound statement a little like the class definitions in that it has a line of code followed by a pair of braces that contain statements.

In this case the line of code starts with the Java keyword, if, and it is followed by a conditional expression in brackets, then the block of code that is to be executed only if the condition is true is added in braces. So a simple example might be

```
if (x>y){
    difference = x-y;
}
```

If the expression x>y is true the code statement difference=x-y is executed. Otherwise the program just ignores this block of code and goes on to the next statement.

We can be a little more precise by using a combination of two keywords, if and else,

```
if (x>y){
    difference = x-y;
}
else{
```

```
    difference = y-x;
}
```

This would ensure that the variable, difference, always has a positive or zero value. It is never given a negative one.

Or we can go further and use the combination, if and else if, as in

```
if (x>y){
    difference = x-y;
}
else if (y>x){
    difference = y-x;
}
```

This would ensure that difference always has a positive value or is unchanged from whatever it was before. This time it cannot be given a zero value.

And finally a word about notation. In Java, the braces are only required if there is more than one statement to be executed. So the above code can be written as

```
if (x>y)  difference = x-y;
else if (y>x)  difference = y-x;
```

This is not generally regarded as good practice but it does present the structure very clearly so it will be used frequently in this book.

Compound Conditions

The simple conditions can be combined to form compound conditions which are sometime difficult to understand but always very useful.

Suppose, for example, we have two figures drawn on the screen and we want to find out if they are overlapping. Then we can use two variables, sepX and sepY to represent the difference between their x and y positions and compare these with the size of the figures.

We can do this in an expression such as,

if (sepX<size && sepY<size){ }

This uses a condition, sepX<size, to see if their x separation is less than their size and another condition, sepY<size, to see if their y separation is less than their size. If both are true, that is, the first and the second condition, they must be overlapping.

This expression uses a new operator, &&, consisting of two ampersand characters. The combination is usually described as an AND operator.

The whole condition is true if both the separate conditions are true. If one or both is not true it fails. In this example the test is to see if two figures are within one size length of each other in terms of both the x separation and the y separation. This means they must be overlapping.

The && operator is sometimes described as a logical or a Boolean operator. There are other such operators but we will only use one of them, namely the | | operator. This too is a double character but in this case it uses the vertical slash character usually found at the bottom left corner of your keyboard, sometimes depicted as a broken vertical line. This is usually described as an OR operator.

> if (sepX>size || sepY>size){ }

The effect of an OR operator is to return a true value for a compound condition in which at least one of the conditions is true. So one or the other must be true. If both are true it returns a true value but if neither is true it returns a false value.

So, if you think about it, the OR expression above, using > operators, has the same effect as the previous AND expression, that used < operators.

One point to note here is that in evaluating these compound expressions we have to know which parts to evaluate first. The rule is that the conditional operators, such as >, <, == and so on always take precedence over the logical ones so we test the sepX<size and sepY<size before we combine them with the &&. This is similar to the precedence rules of arithmetic operations where brackets are evaluated first, then multiply and divide, then add and subtract.

Creating the App

You have to go through the usual procedure. Create a new app. Call it Drawing and the package name com.androidjavaapps.drawing. Then create a new class, Figure, as before.

The starting code is the code used in the previous Graphic app. So you can copy the code from MainActivity.java and Figure.java into the new app, replacing the skeleton code provided by the IDE. Of course, you have to make sure the copying does not overprint the package name which should still refer to drawing.

So we end up with two files, MainActivity.java and Figure,java in the new project java directory, both of which have to be edited. The MainActivity.java contains the ShapeView class that has to have the title bar removed, be scaled to the screen size, and deal with reorientation of the device. The Figure class has to create a new figure, this time of a car, and be directly reusable by ShapeView without any modification to that class.

You might find that the IDE gives an error warning at this point. This is because it can't find the Figure class because it hasn't been coded yet. So you only have to carry on to that stage.

Removing the Title Bar

You may have notice that the previous apps had a black bar across the top of the display containing some device information or the name of the app. This takes up space on the screen, changing its size slightly, and it does not really look like a professionally designed app. So we will remove it.

This is done by adding some code to the onCreate() method, which now becomes

```
@Override
public void onCreate(Bundle savedInstanceState) {
    super.onCreate(savedInstanceState);
    this.requestWindowFeature(Window.FEATURE_NO_TITLE);
    getWindow().setFlags(WindowManager.LayoutParams.
        FLAG_FULLSCREEN,
    WindowManager.LayoutParams.FLAG_FULLSCREEN);
    shapeView=new ShapeView(this);
    setContentView(shapeView);
}
```

The additional statements are

```
this.requestWindowFeature(Window.FEATURE_NO_TITLE);
getWindow().setFlags(WindowManager.LayoutParams.
      FLAG_FULLSCREEN,
WindowManager.LayoutParams.FLAG_FULLSCREEN);
```

These call an Activity method of "this" view object, requestWindowFeature. Its argument is a constant attribute of the Window class, FEATURE_NO_TITLE. Then it uses another method, getWindow of the activity to setFlags(). This takes two identical arguments of the type, WindowsManagerLayoutParams. These are again constants, FLAG_FULLSCREEN. The whole code requests a full screen display with no title bar and invariably gets it. Fortunately you don't have to understand the code to use it.

Scaling the Display

Another feature of our apps so far that makes them unprofessional is that they look different in different screen sizes. To make them look the same on all devices we need to draw them to a scale that is related to the current screen dimensions.

We do this by adding some code to the ShapeView constructor. This becomes

```
public ShapeView(Context context) {
   super(context);
   float w=getResources().getDisplayMetrics().widthPixels;
   float h=getResources().getDisplayMetrics().heightPixels;
   int n=1;
   float size;
   if (w<h) size=w/n;
```

```
    else size= h/n;
    float x=w/2;
    float y=h/2;
    int c=Color.rgb(250,150,0);     // orange color
    int ch=Color.rgb(200,200,0);   // light highlight
    int background=Color.rgb(40, 150, 250);   // grey blue
    setBackgroundColor(background);
    figure=new Figure(size, x, y, c, ch);
}
```

Two new floats, w and h are introduced. These represent the width and height of the display and are obtained from an inherited View method, getResources. This returns an object whose method, getDisplayMetrics then returns variables, widthPixels and heightPixels which contain the width and height of the screen. Again, it is not really necessary to fully understand this code in order to use it but it is a good example of methods returning values which are then used to run other methods in a chained sequence of method calls.

We use these values of w and h to scale our drawing by using another additional variable, n. This is a scaling factor. It is used to scale the drawing size to w/n or h/n, whichever is the smaller. In this case, the value of n is just 1 so the drawing is the same size as the screen width or height. In later apps we will be able to use higher values of n to reduce the size of the figure to a smaller fixed fraction of the screen size. So this deals with the scaling.

The positioning is also made relative to the device screen size by simply assigning x and y, the values w/2 and h/2 so it should be in the middle of the screen, whatever size it is. However, this raises a question of what exactly is meant by the position of the figure. Should x and y refer to the top left corner of the figure or to its center. To make the figure completely reusable we have to reach some sort of agreement here. So we will use the center of the figure as its reference point and always draw the figure on that basis. So this deals with the relative positioning of the figure.

Orientation

When the user rotates a device from one orientation to another, for example, from the normal portrait mode to landscape mode, the display changes. This is because the re-orientation of the screen stops the app and restarts it in the landscape mode. Now the drawing unit size will relate to a larger width so the scaling and positioning of the figure will both change.

This is illustrated in Figure 3 which shows the app displayed in landscape mode with no correction made for the effects of reorientation.

Figure 3. The Drawing app in landscape mode uncorrected.

We can fix this in one of two ways,

- We can fix the screen in portrait or landscape mode so that the display does not rotate. Some apps do this and we will do the same later in the book but it is not necessary here.

- We can set the size of the figure to relate to the width, w, of the screen or the height, h, depending on which of these is the smaller. In portrait mode, w is smaller than h. In landscape mode h is smaller than w. We can do this quite easily by using a Java Decision.

For the latter approach we only have to add two new lines of code to the ShapeView constructor,

```
if (w<h) size=w/n;
else size= h/n;
```

This is a Java decision and it tests to see if the width, w, which we have just obtained, is less than the height, h, of the device screen. If it is, the device is currently being held in portrait mode and we assign the size parameter to w/n. If the condition is not true, it is in landscape mode and we assign size to h/n. So the size is always related to the smaller screen dimension and remains the same when the device is rotated.

The last option will include w == h but this is OK since it would mean there is a square screen and the choice is not important.

You may notice that this decision structure is not laid out exactly the same as the examples given above. Here we have only one statement for each condition so we don't need the braces. Also they are short statements so we have placed them on the same lines as their conditions. This is not strictly the best practice but it makes for clearer logic in a book page so it is used here.

The Activity Code

So with these modifications, the full activity code is

```
public class MainActivity extends Activity {

  ShapeView shapeView;

  @Override
  protected void onCreate(Bundle savedInstanceState) {
    super.onCreate(savedInstanceState);
    this.requestWindowFeature(Window.FEATURE_NO_TITLE);
     getWindow().setFlags(WindowManager.LayoutParams.
        FLAG_FULLSCREEN,
     WindowManager.LayoutParams.FLAG_FULLSCREEN);
    shapeView=new ShapeView(this);
    setContentView(shapeView);
  }

  public class ShapeView extends View{
    Figure figure;

    public ShapeView(Context context){
      super(context);
      float w=getResources().getDisplayMetrics().widthPixels;
      float h=getResources().getDisplayMetrics().heightPixels;
      int n=1;
      float size;
      if (w<h) size=w/n;
      else size= h/n;
      float x=w/2;
      float y=h/2;
      int c=Color.rgb(250,150,40);    // orange color
      int ch=Color.rgb(200,200,200);  // light highlight
      int background=Color.rgb(100, 200, 250);   // grey blue
      setBackgroundColor(background);
      figure=new Figure(size,x,y,c,ch);   // constructor
    }
```

```
    public void onDraw(Canvas canvas){
       figure.draw(canvas);
    }
  }
}
```

A Car Figure

The remaining task is to rewrite the Figure class. This time we will draw a figure of a small car using a Path object. It has to be drawn using the size parameter to scale it to the view and it must be drawn at a position x, y which represents the center of the drawing. Otherwise, it can do anything that gets the drawing done.

```
package com.androidjavaapps.drawing;

import android.graphics.*;

public class Figure {
    float size, x, y;
    int c, ch;
    Paint paint =new Paint();
    float u;
    Path path;

    public Figure(float size, float x, float y, int c, int ch){
        this.size=size;
        this.x=x;
        this.y=y;
        this.c=c;
        this.ch=ch;
        u=size/50;    // relate u to figure size
        path=new Path();
    }

    public void draw(Canvas canvas){
```

```
paint.setStyle(Paint.Style.FILL);
path.moveTo(x-17*u,y-10*u);
path.lineTo(x,y-10*u);
path.lineTo(x+10*u, y);
path.lineTo(x+18*u,y);
path.lineTo(x+20*u,y+10*u);
path.lineTo(x-20*u,y+10*u);
path.close();
paint.setColor(c);
canvas.drawPath(path, paint);
paint.setStyle(Paint.Style.STROKE);
paint.setColor(Color.rgb(50,50,50));
paint.setStrokeWidth(u);
canvas.drawPath(path, paint);
paint.setStyle(Paint.Style.FILL);
canvas.drawCircle(x-10*u, y+10*u, 5*u,paint);
canvas.drawCircle(x+10*u, y+10*u, 5*u,paint);
path.reset();
//back window
path.moveTo(x-15*u,y-8*u);
path.lineTo(x-10*u,y-8*u);
path.lineTo(x-10*u,y);
path.lineTo(x-16*u,y);
//front window
path.moveTo(x-8*u, y-8*u);
path.lineTo(x-1*u,y-8*u);
path.lineTo(x+7*u,y);
path.lineTo(x-8*u,y);
path.close();
canvas.drawPath(path,paint);
paint.setColor(ch);
canvas.drawCircle(x-10*u, y+10*u, 2*u,paint);
canvas.drawCircle(x+10*u, y+10*u, 2*u,paint);
    }
}
```

In order to draw the figure to the required scale we have introduced a Path variable, path, and a new variable, u, both declared in the instance variables and initialized in the constructor, as usual. The variable, u, is a drawing unit and it is assigned the value of size/50. Then the drawing coordinates are all presented as multiples of u so the drawing is scaled to the value of size and completely independent of the size and resolution of the device screen. In this case, each picture element is 1/50 of the size parameter passed from ShapeView but we could make it any fraction we want. A more detailed figure, for example, might need something like 1/100 or 1/1000 of size.

So the figure is an independent, reusable and easily replaceable class. We only have to decide what the reference coordinates, x and y, should relate to. In this case we have already decided that it should be the center point of the figure, so we will draw around that point.

The Draw() Method

The draw() method starts by setting the Style to FILL then defines a path to represent the outline of the car. It draws around a central x, y point so the x values are from -20 to +20 leaving some space on each side. The y-values are not so precise but still centered near the mid-point. Then it sets the color to (250, 150, 0) which is an orange color and draws the path.

```
public void draw(){
    paint.setStyle(Paint.Style.FILL);
    path.moveTo(x-17*u,y-10*u);
    path.lineTo(x,y-10*u);
    path.lineTo(x+10*u, y);
    path.lineTo(x+18*u,y);
    path.lineTo(x+20*u,y+10*u);
    path.lineTo(x-20*u,y+10*u);
    path.close();
    paint.setColor(Color.rgb(250,150,0));
    canvas.drawPath(path, paint);
```

Then it redraws the same path after setting the Style to STROKE and the color to (50, 50, 50) and the width to one unit, u, to get a dark grey outline.

```
paint.setStyle(Paint.Style.STROKE);
paint.setColor(Color.rgb(50,50,50));
paint.setStrokeWidth(u);
canvas.drawPath(path, paint);
```

The next part of the drawing resets the Style to FILL and draws two circles to represent the tires of the car in the same dark grey color.

```
paint.setStyle(Paint.Style.FILL);
canvas.drawCircle(x-10*u, y+10*u, 5*u,paint);
canvas.drawCircle(x+10*u, y+10*u, 5*u,paint);
```

Finally the car windows are drawn in a new path. This requires a reset to start a new path definition.

```
path.reset();
//back window
path.moveTo(x-15*u,y-8*u);
path.lineTo(x-10*u,y-8*u);
path.lineTo(x-10*u,y);
path.lineTo(x-16*u,y);
//front window
path.moveTo(x-8*u, y-8*u);
path.lineTo(x-1*u,y-8*u);
path.lineTo(x+7*u,y);
path.lineTo(x-8*u,y);
path.close();
canvas.drawPath(path,paint);
paint.setColor(Color.rgb(200,200,0));
canvas.drawCircle(x-10*u, y+10*u, 2*u,paint);
canvas.drawCircle(x+10*u, y+10*u, 2*u,paint);
}
```

Another Shape

If you have not been coding this app as we go along now is the time to try it. This is the best way to learn how to write real code and to find out if you enjoy the frustrations and elations of programming.

You should try to create a new Figure class to replace the car drawing and see what you can do. And if you are not coding along then you can try to imagine what the code would look like.

7. Patterns

The Aim

The aim of this app is to draw several figures on the screen in a regular array. This pattern could be used as a background for an app but in this case it is being used simply to demonstrate Java loops and arrays, which we will use in later apps.

There are several types of loop and we will study two of them at this stage, the for loop and the while loop. The other two are the switch case structure, which we will look at later, and the foreach loop.

We will extend the previous app to a new app called Array and a package, com.androidjavaapps.array by modifying the MainActivity and Figure classes of the Drawing app.

What we are looking for is something like Figure 1.

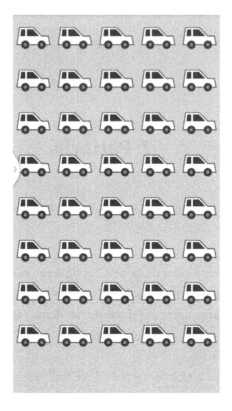

Figure 1. An array of car figures

For Loops

A loop repeats a number of program statements for a certain number of iterations, or cycles. It is a way of writing a few lines of code and having them run many times. It is useful for repetitive tasks that otherwise might require an enormous number of statements.

In the "for" loop, the number of iterations is known beforehand at the programming stage and can be written into the statement.

It has a structure as in the following example:-

```
for (int index = 0; index < 100; index=index+1) {
        x=x+20;
        y=y+30;
}
```

As for the decision structure discussed in the previous chapter, this starts with a conditional expression in parentheses but this time it is a rather complicated structure comprising three linked terms separated by semicolons. This is followed by the block of code that has to be executed. The execution is related to the conditions but this time the program loops back after each execution and tests the conditions again. This is repeated until the conditions give a false return. So the block of code is repeated a fixed number of times.

The first term inside the brackets, int index = 0, is actually a declaration and initialization of a new variable. Here we have called it index but it can be any variable. The variable could have been declared outside the, for, structure, and used previously, in which case the int keyword would not be required and it would be a simple assignment rather than a declaration.

The second term, index < 100, defines the limit if the iterations. In this case, it repeats as long as the value of index is less than 100. As soon as it hits 100 the looping stops and the program continues on to the next statement in the program.

The third term describes how the value of index is to change from one iteration to the next. In this case it is to be incremented by 1, by assigning the value of index to its current value plus 1. It can be changed in any systematic way. For example it can be decremented from some large starting value or multiplied by some constant but incrementing is probably the most common operation.

This example instructs the program to give index a starting value of 0 then increment it by one until its value equals 100. The block of code will be executed for values 0 to 99, that is, 100 times. And when the loop ends, index will have a value of 100.

In each iteration it will assign the value of some variable, x, to its current value plus 20, and assign the value of a variable, y, to its current value plus 30. This is something we covered in chapter 2 but there is a shorter way of executing these assignment operations that we should introduce now, since they are always used for looping.

- x=x+1 can be written as x++.
- x=x-1 can be written as x---.
- x=x+20 can be written as x+=20.
- x=x+30 can be written as x+=20.
- x=x*4 can be written as x*=4.
- x=x/4 can be written as x/=4.

And there are lots of other examples that can be used with other operators and other variables instead of the constants used in these examples. So the above code example is usually written as

```
for (int index = 0; index < 100; index++) {
        x+=20;
        y+=30;
}
```

While Loops

The main alternative to the for loop is the while loop. It does not prescribe the number of iterations since this is not known until the program is actually running. This time, a block of statements will be repeated as long as some condition remains true, which is determined as a result of the code being executed in the loop itself. The structure is again that of a condition in brackets followed by the block of code to be repeated. For example,

```
while (y <h ) {
    y+=30;
}
```

This will increment the value of y as long as it is less than h. When it becomes greater than or equal to h the program exits from the loop and goes on to the next statement.

Java Arrays

To take full advantage of program loops we need to use Array variables. In fact, one of the main reasons for using loops is to process arrays.

An array is a Java class that represents a collection of indexed variables that are usually processed together and do not require individual names. They are described by a single name and a numerical index. In Java, as in most programming languages, this index is placed in square brackets and always starts at 0.

However, an Array, like a String which we will discuss later, is an unusual class in that it is defined in the Java language rather than the Android system or by the programmer. As a result its usage is slightly different from other classes.

As an example we might have an array of int variables score[] representing a set of scores. So score[0] would be the first element, then score[1] would be the next in the list and score[2] next, and so on.

We could have an array of Figure objects called figure[] and consisting of figure[0], figure[1], figure[2], and so on. Each element is an object of the class Figure with the common class behavior but its own set of attribute values.

More generally, a single element of this array would be described as

figure[index]

where index is an integer with the values 0, 1, 2, 3, 4, 5, and so on.

Declaring Arrays

An array can be declared in several ways. However, to keep the theory as simple as possible, only two of these will be used here. Both use the square brackets and the variable type it contains to declare an array but then they initialize differently.

The first approach declares an array with the variable type followed by empty square brackets and assigns this to a new array of the same type with square brackets containing the number of elements in the array. For example an array of ints might be

int [ ] scores = new int[10];

And a new array of 20 Figures might be

Figure [ ] figures = new Figure[20];

112

Note that we always have to state how many elements will be in the array, that is, its length, but we do not have to say what they are at this stage. There are other array classes in Java that do permit unsized arrays but these will not be used here.

Then, to initialize the values of the array elements we have to go through each in turn. For simple variables it is a straightforward process, for example,

scores[0] = 25;
scores[1] = 34;

However, for an array of objects, each object has to be created, for example,

figure[0] = new Figure(size, x, y);
figure[1] = new Figure(size, x, y);

The advantage of placing our figures in an array is that we can use a single loop to process all of them, say, from figure[0] to figure[19] in the same way, for example, to resize the figures or move them to different positions. This is exactly what we are going to do in our apps.

The above method of initializing arrays is particularly suited to looping through an array of objects. If we are dealing with an array of numbers, there is a quicker way to do the initializing. This uses braces to contain the starting values,

int [ ] scores = {25, 30, 23, 10, 40};

The Array class also has a number of useful attributes and methods but we will only be using one of these, namely, the length attribute.

The length of an array is the number of elements it contains and is given, for example, by

scores.length for the scores array or
figures.length for the figures array.

We will use these as the limits of for loops to process arrays instead of hard coding some value such as 20 into the loop. Although we know how many elements there are, it is better to write code that does not have to be changed if the number of elements is changed.

We mostly use for loops to process arrays since the length is known but sometimes it is easier to use a while loop and both can be illustrated in the Pattern app.

A Pattern App

We can extend the Drawing app to draw many figures in a new Pattern app by using arrays. We will modify the ShapeView class to draw an array of figures that fill the screen and redo the figure to draw a house. So we should end up with a picture consisting of an array of houses.

So once again we can start by creating a new app, this time called Pattern. Again we copy the code from the previous Drawing app into this one then modify it and check the package name refers to pattern.

Then the activity class becomes,

package com.androidjavaapps.pattern;

import android.os.*;
import android.app.*;

```java
import android.view.*;
import android.content.*;
import android.graphics.*;

public class MainActivity extends Activity {

  ShapeView shapeView;

  @Override
  protected void onCreate(Bundle savedInstanceState) {
    super.onCreate(savedInstanceState);
    this.requestWindowFeature(Window.FEATURE_NO_TITLE);
     getWindow().setFlags(WindowManager.LayoutParams.
       FLAG_FULLSCREEN,
     WindowManager.LayoutParams.FLAG_FULLSCREEN);
    shapeView=new ShapeView(this);
    setContentView(shapeView);
  }

  public class ShapeView extends View{
    Figure[] figure;

    public ShapeView(Context context){
      super(context);
      float w=getResources().getDisplayMetrics().widthPixels;
      float h=getResources().getDisplayMetrics().heightPixels;
      int n=5;
      float size;
      if (w<h) size=w/n;
      else size= h/n;
      float x=w/2;
      float y=h/2;
      int c=Color.rgb(250,150,40);    // orange color
      int ch=Color.rgb(200,200,200);   // light highlight
      int background=Color.rgb(100, 200, 250);  // grey blue
      setBackgroundColor(background);
      int elements=n;
      figure = new Figure[elements];
      for (int i=0; i<figure.length;i++){
```

```
        x=size/2+size*i;
        y=h/2;
        figure[i]=new Figure(size, x, y, c, ch);
         }
       }

    public void onDraw(Canvas canvas){
        for(int i=0;i<figure.length;i++){
        figure[i].draw(canvas);
         }
       }
     }
   }
```

So we declare an array of figures called figure and initialize it in the constructor with a variable, elements, to represent the number of elements. We have also increased the value of n to 5 so the size is 1/5 of the screen width and elements is given the value n so there should be an array of 5 elements across the screen.

These are initialized in the loop

```
for (int i=0; i<figure.length;i++){
    x=size/2+size*i;
    y=h/2;
    figure[i]=new Figure(size, x, y, c, ch);
}
```

Here the x value, which is again the center of the figure starts at size/2 for the index, i =0, then increments by size*i for each i value. This will spread the array evenly across the screen, creating a new figure at each position.

The onDraw() method is also changed to draw the figures using a similar loop

```
for(int i=0;i<figure.length;i++){
    figure[i].draw(canvas);
```

}.

This draws a row of 5 Figures across the mid-point of the screen as illustrated in Figure 2.

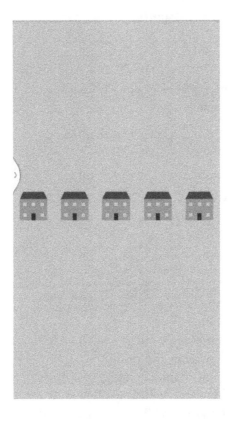

Figure 2. An array of figures drawn across the screen

The Figure Class

The Figure class required to draw a house is

package com.androidjavaapps.pattern;

```java
import android.graphics.*;

public class Figure {
    float size, x, y;
    int c, ch;
    Paint paint =new Paint();
    float u;
    Path path;

    public Figure(float size, float x, float y, int c, int ch){
        this.size=size;
        this.x=x;
        this.y=y;
        this.c=c;
        this.ch=ch;
        u=size/100;   // relate u to figure size
        path=new Path();
    }

    public void draw(Canvas canvas){
        paint.setStyle(Paint.Style.FILL);
        // draw the body of the house centered on x, y
        paint.setColor(c);
        canvas.drawRect(x-40*u, y-30*u,x+40*u, y+30*u, paint);
        //draw windows and door
        paint.setColor(Color.rgb(50, 50, 50));
        canvas.drawRect(x-30*u, y-20*u,x-20*u,y-10*u, paint);
        canvas.drawRect(x+20*u, y-20*u,x+30*u,y-10*u, paint);
        canvas.drawRect(x-5*u, y-20*u,x+5*u,y-10*u, paint);
        canvas.drawRect(x-30*u, y+10*u,x-20*u,y+20*u, paint);
        canvas.drawRect(x+20*u, y+10*u,x+30*u,y+20*u, paint);
        paint.setColor(Color.rgb(50, 150, 100));
        canvas.drawRect(x-6*u, y+10*u,x+6*u,y+30*u, paint);
        //draw roof
        path.moveTo(x-40*u, y-30*u);
        path.lineTo(x-30*u, y-50*u);
        path.lineTo(x+30*u,y-50*u);
        path.lineTo(x+30*u, y-50*u);
```

```
        path.lineTo(x+40*u, y-30*u);
        path.close();
        paint.setColor(ch);
        canvas.drawPath(path, paint);
    }
}
```

This time we draw on a grid of 100 units, so the unit variable, u=100. The drawing uses only FILL style with no outlines. It first draws the body of a house as a rectangle from x-40 to x+40 leaving some space at the edges of the 100 by 100 drawing surface. The house body is drawn in the color, c, transferred from ShapeView.

The code then sets the color to a fixed value of light grey to draw four rectangles for the windows and sets the color to a green shade for a door rectangle. These colors have to be fixed since we are using the color parameters c and ch for the house and its roof. If we want to have more color selection from ShapeView we will have to change its code and the Figure constructor. For now, we will make do with two adjustable colors.

Finally the roof is drawn as a path and given the fill color, ch.

The Complete Pattern

The next example is a little more difficult. We would like to draw a series of rows to fill the entire screen. The simplest way to do this is to create an array of sub-arrays. Each sub array would be a row across the screen and the outer array would be an array of these rows. We can use a two-dimensional array of figures. These will be indexed j, i where i represents the position on each row and j is the row number. The loop goes down the rows from j=0 to j=maxRows and in each of these loops an inner loop goes from i=0 to i=

rowElements. We are placing the j index before the i index because it is easier to imagine the drawing on a row by row basis down the screen, that is, the second dimension looping faster than the first one.

So we need a two dimensional array, Figures[][] where the first index is j for the row number and the second index is i for the row position. We also need to declare two array dimension, maxRows, the number of rows, and row Elements, the number of figures in each row. These are declared as instance variables since they can only be initialized in the constructor, to create the array, but also have to be used in the onDraw() method to draw it.

The array is declared as a double array in the constructor and drawn in the onDraw() method using two index variables, j for the row number and i, for the number in each row. If we use int i=0 to start the i loop it would mean repeatedly reusing a variable name which is not allowed. So we have to declare the i variable outside the loops. We also try to spread the figures evenly, one size apart in both directions.

The final outcome is shown in Figure 3.

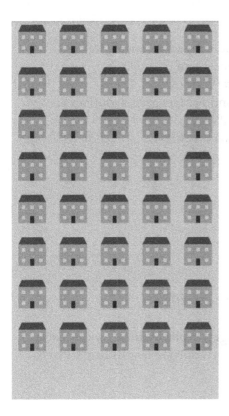

Figure 3. A two dimensional array of house figures

The full code for the MainActivity file is

package com.androidjavaapps.pattern;

import android.os.*;
import android.app.*;
import android.view.*;
import android.content.*;
import android.graphics.*;

public class MainActivity extends Activity {

    ShapeView shapeView;

```
@Override
protected void onCreate(Bundle savedInstanceState) {
   super.onCreate(savedInstanceState);
   this.requestWindowFeature(Window.FEATURE_NO_TITLE);
    getWindow().setFlags(WindowManager.LayoutParams.
       FLAG_FULLSCREEN,
    WindowManager.LayoutParams.FLAG_FULLSCREEN);
   shapeView=new ShapeView(this);
   setContentView(shapeView);
}

public class ShapeView extends View{
   Figure[][] figure;
   int maxRows, rowElements;

   public ShapeView(Context context){
      super(context);
      float w=getResources().getDisplayMetrics().widthPixels;
      float h=getResources().getDisplayMetrics().heightPixels;
      int n=5;
      float size,x,y;
      if (w<h) size=w/n;
      else size= h/n;
      int c=Color.rgb(250,250, 200);     // house color
      int ch=Color.rgb(200,100, 50);   // light highlight
      int background=Color.rgb(100, 200, 250);   // grey blue
      setBackgroundColor(background);
      rowElements=n;
      maxRows=(int) (h/size);
      int i=0;
      figure = new Figure[maxRows][rowElements];
      for (int j=0; j<maxRows; j++){
        for(i=0; i<rowElements; i++){
           x=size/2+size*i;
           y=size/2+size*j;
           figure[j][i]=new Figure(size, x, y, c, ch);
        }
      }
   }
```

```
public void onDraw(Canvas canvas){
    int i;
    for(int j=0; j<maxRows; j++){
      for(i=0; i<rowElements; i++){
         figure[j][i].draw(canvas);
        }
      }
   }
  }
}
```

There is a bit of a gap at the bottom of the array because the division of h by size did not lead to an exact result, as expected, but rounded down to an integer. We could add more code to deal with this but it is not worth the effort at this stage. Instead we will go on to another way of placing multiple figures on the screen.

What Next

If you would like to practice you might try to draw a few different array sizes and matching figure sizes and see how they fit into the screen of your device. You could also copy some other figure into the Figure class and draw an array of these.

Bill Tait

8. Calculation

The Aim

The aim is to produce a Picture app that will fill the screen with figures in some distribution other than an array. This time we will use a mathematical function to produce the distribution. We will still have to use an array to hold the figures but we will find a different way to arrange them on the screen.

We will also draw another version of Figure, this time to show a face.

So the idea is to display the figures randomly scattered about the screen instead of in a fixed array. Random effects are key features of many games and we can have a look at them now.

A Random Picture

We can reuse much of the previous app but we only need a one dimensional array to hold a lot of figures and we can make this any size we like. Then we just use the Math class to generate a few random x and y positions to populate the array then draw it as usual.

However, there are some new problems in keeping the figures within the boundaries of the screen and preventing them from overlapping. These also need some Math methods.

The Math Class

The Math class, like the Color class, does not have objects since they would all be the same. So its methods are all static class methods. These can be used for many purposes such as

Math.abs(n) to calculate the absolute (positive) value of n

Math.sin(theta) to calculate the sine of the angle theta.

Math.cos(theta) to calculate the cosine of the angle theta.

Math.round(x) to round a float to the nearest integer value.

There are also some constants, such as Math.PI which has the value of the pi constant

However, we will use only one Math method to start with, namely,

Math.random() which produces and returns a double precision, pseudo random number between 0 and 1.0. It is generated by a software algorithm so it is not truly random but it is near enough for most programming purposes. So,

x=Math.random();   returns a value of 0 to 1.0 to the variable x.

x=Math,random() * 100; returns a value of between 0 and 100 to x.

We can use this approach to generate random screen positions for our Figure objects.

Generating Random Positions

We need a one dimensional array to hold the figures. We can call this figure[]. We also need a Figure class to define the elements of the array and we can keep things really simple by just rewriting the house figure from the previous app to produce the figure of a face.

So the ShapeView class declares a one dimensional array of Figures in the instance variables and initializes the array in the constructor. Then it populates the array with

```
int elements=20;
figure = new Figure[elements];
for(int i=0; i<figure.length; i++){
    x=(float) (size/2+Math.random()*w);
    y=(float) (size/2+Math.random()*h);
    figure[i]=new Figure(size, x, y, c, ch);
}
```

By using figure.length as the limit of the for loop both here and in the onDraw() method we do not have to make the variable, elements an instance variable so we declare it and initialize it to a value of 20 in the constructor..

In the loop the math is straightforward. We simply set each x and y value to a random number equal to the width and height, respectively, plus half a size length to stop it overlapping with the side and top of the screen.

But there is a complication because we are now mixing data types. We have a mixture of double and float variables on the right of each assignment statement but we want a float on the left. Since we are demoting a double to a float we need to explicitly cast the value of the entire expression to a float. If we did not think of this beforehand the IDE will certainly point out our error.

The Figure Class

The new Figure code uses a scale of 80 units. It draws a filled circle for a face then two circle for the eyes and smaller circles for the pupils. Then it uses a path to draw a mouth. It resets the path each time draw is called to ensure a new path is started instead of extending the mouth of the previous figure.

The complete code is

```
package com.androidjavaapps.picture;

import android.graphics.*;

public class Figure {
    float size, x, y, vx, vy;
    float r, u;
    int c, ch;
    Paint paint =new Paint();
    float w,h;
    Path path;
    int count, start, frame, frames, rate;

    public Figure(float size, float x, float y, int c, int ch) {
        this.size = size;
        this.x = x;
```

```
    this.y = y;
    r = size / 2;
    u = size / 80;
    this.c = c;
    this.ch = ch;
    path = new Path();
}

public void draw(Canvas canvas){
    paint.setStyle(Paint.Style.FILL);
    // draw round face
    paint.setColor(c);
    canvas.drawCircle(x, y, 40*u, paint);
    //draw two circles for whites of eyes
    paint.setColor(Color.rgb(200, 200, 200));
    canvas.drawCircle(x-17*u, y-6*u, 14*u, paint);
    canvas.drawCircle(x+17*u, y-6*u, 14*u, paint);
    //draw blue pupils at same points
    paint.setColor(Color.rgb(0, 100, 200));
    canvas.drawCircle(x-17*u, y-4*u, 7*u, paint);
    canvas.drawCircle(x+17*u, y-4*u, 7*u, paint);//straight
    // draw the mouth
    path.reset();
    path.moveTo(x-24*u, y+16*u);
    path.lineTo(x-12*u, y+18*u);
    path.lineTo(x,y+20*u);
    path.lineTo(x+12*u, y+18*u);
    path.lineTo(x+24*u, y+16*u);
    path.lineTo(x+10*u,y+24*u);
    path.lineTo(x,y+26*u);
    path.lineTo(x-10*u,y+24*u);
    path.close();
    paint.setColor(ch);
    canvas.drawPath(path, paint);
```

```
    }
}
```

The First Version of Picture

With the modofications described above the MainActivity code is

```java
package com.androidjavaapps.picture;

import android.os.*;
import android.app.*;
import android.view.*;
import android.content.*;
import android.graphics.*;

public class MainActivity extends Activity {

    ShapeView shapeView;

    @Override
    protected void onCreate(Bundle savedInstanceState) {
        super.onCreate(savedInstanceState);
        this.requestWindowFeature(Window.FEATURE_NO_TITLE);
         getWindow().setFlags(WindowManager.LayoutParams.
            FLAG_FULLSCREEN,
          WindowManager.LayoutParams.FLAG_FULLSCREEN);
        shapeView=new ShapeView(this);
        setContentView(shapeView);
    }

    public class ShapeView extends View{
        Figure[] figure;

        public ShapeView(Context context){
            super(context);
            float w=getResources().getDisplayMetrics().widthPixels;
```

```
    float h=getResources().getDisplayMetrics().heightPixels;
    int n=5;
    float size,x,y;
    if (w<h) size=w/n;
    else size= h/n;
    int c=Color.rgb(250,250, 200);     // first color
    int ch=Color.rgb(200,100, 50);   // second color
    int background=Color.rgb(100, 200, 250);   // grey blue
    setBackgroundColor(background);
    int elements=20;
    figure = new Figure[elements];
    for(int i=0; i<figure.length; i++){
        x=(float) (size/2+Math.random()*w);
        y=(float) (size/2+Math.random()*h);
        figure[i]=new Figure(size, x, y, c, ch);
    }
}

public void onDraw(Canvas canvas){
    for(int i=0; i<figure.length; i++){
        figure[i].draw(canvas);
    }
}
}
}
```

The result of running this app is illustrated in Figure 1.

Clearly there are two things wrong with this picture. First some of the figures are partly off screen and second, some of them are overlapping. So we now have to solve these problems.

Figure 1. A random distribution of Figures.

Keeping the Figures on the Screen

The first one is easily solved. We have been generating random numbers within the range of the full width and height of the screen. The x and y measurements are to the center of each figure and already we have added size/2 to our random positions so they should all be clear of the top and left sides of the screen. We need to do the same for the other sides. So we reduce the random range from w to w-size and from h to h-size. With the size/2 increment at the start of the calculation, this leaves the maximum positions at least size/2 inside the screen. This gives us

```
for (int i=0; i<figure.length; i++){
    x= (float)(size/2+Math.random()*(w-size));
    y=(float)(size/2+Math.random()*(h-size));
    figure[i]=new Figure(size, x, y, c, ch);
}
```

This works fine and none of the figures is out of the screen. But they still overlap with each other and this is a much more difficult problem to solve.

Preventing Overlap

The best way to deal with it is to check, for each pair of x and y values, if they are within a half size of any of the others and, if so, reject them.

We can do this, without making the loop very complicated by using a new method, checkSeparation(). It can be a private function since it will only be used by the ShapeView constructor. It will return a boolean variable called separated and if this is true, the two figures being compared are separated. In that case, a new figure is created. Otherwise the loop just continues to test new locations, but first the index is decremented so that when the loop moves on and the i value is incremented it is effectively still at the same position and trying again to get a valid figure position.

The checkSeparation(method is quite complicated. It receives the current values of size, x, y and i. It will loop through all the figures already accepted, that is, from 0 to i-1 and test the difference between the x values and the y values. If the x separation and the y separation between the proposed new figure and any of the existing ones are both within one size value of each other they are touching and the test fails.

133

The final code is

```
private boolean checkSeparation(float size, float x, float y, int i ){
    float sepX, sepY;
    for(int j=0; j<i; j++){
        sepX=Math.abs(x-figure[j].x);
        sepY=Math.abs(y-figure[j].y);
        if(sepX<size && sepY<size) return false;
    }
    return true;
}
```

It also uses the compound condition described in chapter 6.

```
if(sepX<size && sepY<size) return false;
```

This causes a false value to be returned to the separated variable. The return keyword stops the loop and exits from the method. Back in the constructor the for loop decrements the i value and tries again. The process can fail to create a separated figure several times but eventually it gets through the entire array of figures then it returns a true value to the separated variable and we should have 20 non-overlapping, randomly distributed figures as illustrated in Figure 2.

The Final Code

So the final code for the ShapeView constructor and the checkSeparation method is

```
package com.androidjavaapps.picture;

import android.os.*;
import android.app.*;
```

134

```
import android.view.*;
import android.content.*;
import android.graphics.*;

public class MainActivity extends Activity {

    ShapeView shapeView;

    @Override
    protected void onCreate(Bundle savedInstanceState) {
        super.onCreate(savedInstanceState);
        this.requestWindowFeature(Window.FEATURE_NO_TITLE);
        getWindow().setFlags(WindowManager.LayoutParams.
                FLAG_FULLSCREEN,
            WindowManager.LayoutParams.FLAG_FULLSCREEN);
        shapeView=new ShapeView(this);
        setContentView(shapeView);
    }

public class ShapeView extends View{
    Figure[] figure;

    public ShapeView(Context context){
        super(context);
        float w=getResources().getDisplayMetrics().widthPixels;
        float h=getResources().getDisplayMetrics().heightPixels;
        int n=5;
        float size,x,y;
        if (w<h) size=w/n;
        else size= h/n;
        int c=Color.rgb(250,250, 200);    // first color
        int ch=Color.rgb(200,100, 50);  // second color
        int background=Color.rgb(100, 200, 250);  // grey blue
        setBackgroundColor(background);
        int elements=20;
        figure = new Figure[elements];
        boolean separated=true;
```

```
    for (int i=0; i<figure.length; i++){
    x= (float)(size/2+Math.random()*(w-size));
    y=(float)(size/2+Math.random()*(h-size));
    separated=checkSeparation(size, x, y, i);
    if(separated == true) figure[i]=new Figure(size, x, y, c, ch);
    else i--;
    }
  }


private boolean checkSeparation(float size, float x, float y, int i ){
    float sepX, sepY;
    for(int j=0; j<i; j++){
      sepX=Math.abs(x-figure[j].x);
       sepY=Math.abs(y-figure[j].y);
       if(sepX<size && sepY<size) return false;
    }
    return true;
 }

public void onDraw(Canvas canvas){
    for(int i=0; i<figure.length; i++){
      figure[i].draw(canvas);
    }
 }

 }
 }
```

The outcome from Picture is now as shown in Figure 2.

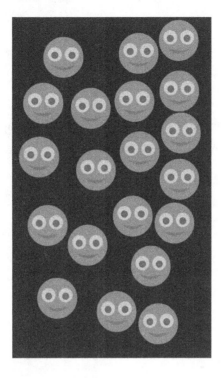

Figure 2. The app with a non-overlapping random distribution

Orientation

We have experienced this problem in previous apps and dealt with it after a fashion. But it is more noticeable in this app. Remember, every time a user rotates the device from a portrait to a landscape orientation (in either direction) the app stops and restarts. Then it generates an entirely new random distribution. So you will find that the distribution of the figures changes each time the orientation is changed.

We mention the problem here but we will not solve it until a later app when it will be important not to change the display when a device is rotated.

What Next

As usual, you are now encouraged to extend the app in some way to make it your own.

9. Motion

The Aim

The aim this time is to create a motion app with a number of figures that are moving about on the screen. It will be an animated version of Picture with moving figures. But we will replace the house figure with a ball figure copied from the Graphic app we developed in Chapter 5, since moving houses are not very credible.

We can create a new app called Movers and copy the code for MainActivity from the Picture app. Then we will create a new version of the Figure class but this time we will call it Sprite. We change the name because we have to make alterations to the code that means it will no longer be a replaceable figure class.

In general programming, a sprite is a user interface class which generates visual objects that move. The ones that don't move are sometimes called widgets.

So we will have an array of balls randomly distributed on the screen. They will move around the screen bouncing off the sides and each other.

But first we need some more Java theory on how to add movement to user interfaces.

A Moving Ball

We can illustrate the motion process by moving just one ball. To do this we have to give the Figure class two more attributes to convert it to a Sprite class. These are the velocity in the x direction and the velocity in the y direction. We can call them vx and vy. Together they describe the speed of movement in any direction. They represent the number of pixels by which the x and y variables change between screen refreshes. So their size determines the total distance covered every time the screen is redrawn, which is the speed of movement.

For example if vx is 8 and vy is 4 a single movement will advance the x position of the ball 8 pixels to the right and the y coordinate 4 pixels downwards. Then a draw() execution will erase the display and redraw the ball at the new position to complete the movement.

So the complete process involves incrementing the x and y variables of the ball by vx and vy then redrawing the screen. If we continually increment the x and y values, in a loop, for example, the ball will appear to move across the screen. This is the same sort of motion that is created in a movie by displaying a series of frames each slightly different from the previous one.

Each ball needs to have its own vx and vy values as well as its x any y coordinates so we have to add the vx and vy parameters to the new Sprite class and its constructor to give them starting values.

The Timer Class

To make the movement take place we need another ShapeView method, move(), which increments the x and y parameters of the sprite by vx and vy. Then a call to sprite.draw() will redraw the ball in its new position. So now the ShapeView object has to call move() to change the position coordinates and then, when onDraw() is run in a screen refresh it will call sprite.draw() as usual, to draw the sprite in its new position.

To get smooth movement we have to do this in a controlled way at regular time intervals. For this we need a Timer object and a TimerTask object so both of these classes must be imported to the program by adding a line

import java.util.*;

Then we use these classes in a quite complicated way. In ShapeView, we declare a Timer object, called timer,

Timer timer;

Then we run the Tmer schedule() method which requires a TimerTask object. However, we are not allowed to create a named object so we have to use an anonymous TimerTask object. This means we create a new object as an argument to the schedule method. In other words we define the constructor inside the method. The structure is as follows:-

timer.schedule(new TimerTask(){ timertask statements},0,10);

So the method requires three arguments, an anonymous TimerTask object then two parameters. The first of these defines the delay in milliseconds before starting to run the task and the second defines the period in milliseconds between successive runs. So this example waits for 0 milliseconds then repeats every 10 milliseconds – forever.

```
timer.schedule(new TimerTask(){
    public void run(){
        runOnUiThread(new Runnable(){
            @Override
            public void run() {
                move();
                invalidate(); //after they have all moved
            }
        });
    }
},0,20);
```

It is not really necessary to fully understand this code in order to use it but essentially it runs an OnUiThread method that creates an anonymous object of the Runnable class and this has a run() method that is overridden to run the code we want to repeat every 10 milliseconds. In this example we will move our figure with the statement

```
sprite.move();
```

But there is one last problem. We can't guarantee a screen refresh after every move so we have to force it. We do this by calling a method of the View class, called invalidate().

This invalidates a property of the user interface thread which forces as screen refresh.

So every 10 milliseconds, in this example, the figure moves its position coordinates then the screen refreshes to show the updated view. The only way to stop the process is to call the timer.cancel() method or stop the app.

So now we have a modified ShapeView class that includes the timer object in its attributes and a sprite object. To test the code we still need a Sprite object

The Sprite Class

We can start by rewriting the Figure class as a new Sprite class. This will have two new attributes, vx and vy and since we are moving towards a finished app we will use the high resolution version of Paint that anti-aliases all the drawings. This takes longer to execute but produces a better result. So the complete Sprite.java file is

```
package com.androidjavaapps.movers;

import android.graphics.*;

public class Sprite {

    float size, x, y, vx, vy;
    float r;      // radius of circle or separation required
    int c, ch;
    RadialGradient radialGradient;
    Paint paint =new Paint(Paint.ANTI_ALIAS_FLAG);

public Sprite(float size, float x, float y, int c, int ch, float vx, float vy){
        this.size=size;
        this.x=x;
        this.y=y;
        this.c=c;
        this.ch=ch;
        this.vx=vx;
        this.vy=vy;
        r=size/2;
    }

    public void draw(Canvas canvas){
        radialGradient = new RadialGradient(x-r/2,y-r/2,r*3/2,
ch,c,Shader.TileMode.CLAMP);
        paint.setShader(radialGradient);
        canvas.drawCircle(x, y, r, paint);
    }
}
```

The draw() Method

The only change to the draw() method is that the radial gradient has to be created new each time the figure is drawn. This is because the movement has just changed the x and y coordinates so it is defined in terms of the previous values of x and y. This does not mean that we are accumulating hundreds of radialGradient objects since each instance replaces the previous one.

In general, it is not a good idea to create a new object in each draw process since it is likely to slow the motion but the alternative leads to an even more complicated code. It would allow a single radial gradient to be created in the constructor but it would have to be moved along with the sprite object, with the same collision and bounce tests. So if you find the motion becomes irregular after running for a while this is the solution you should examine.

The ShapeView Class

This does need substantial changes. As expected, the attributes now include a Sprite class, a Timer class and a TimerTask class. And because of other modification we have had to declare the screen width and height as well as the sprite size here. We are going to use these variables in other methods besides the constructor where they will be initialized as usual.

```
public class ShapeView extends View{
    Sprite[] sprite;
    Timer timer;
    TimerTask timerTask;
    float w, h, size;

    public ShapeView(Context context){
        super(context);
```

```
w=getResources().getDisplayMetrics().widthPixels;
h=getResources().getDisplayMetrics().heightPixels;
int n=6;
if (w<h) size=w/n;
else size= h/n;
int c=Color.rgb(180,120,50);
int ch=Color.rgb(200,200,200);
int background=Color.rgb(40, 50, 60);
setBackgroundColor(background);
int elements=16;
sprite = new Sprite[elements];
setup(c, ch);
```

The constructor is changed slightly to initialize a sprite instead of a figure and values of n=6 and elements = 16 are assigned. However, the main change is that some of the code that was used to set up the view is now delegated to a new setup() method. This is because the constructor is becoming quite complicated and this strategy should help to clarify it.

The Setup() Method

All the code that was used to set up the random distribution of figures, and now sprites, is relocated in this method. It was already complicated but now it also has to initialize vx and vy so it is transferred to a separate method. As before, it also calls a checkSeparation() method. You should recognize most of the code.

```
public void setup(int c, int ch){
    boolean separated=true;
    double direction;
    float x, y, vx, vy, vxMax=4, vyMax=4;
    for (int i=0; i<sprite.length; i++){
        x= (float)(size/2+Math.random()*(w-size));
        y=(float)(size/2+Math.random()*(h-size));
        vx=(float) Math.random()*vxMax+1;
```

```
        direction= Math.random()-0.5;
        if(direction<0)vx=-vx; // to get negative directions
        vy=(float) Math.random()*vyMax+1;
        direction= Math.random()-0.5;
        if(direction<0)vy=-vy;
        separated = checkSeparation(size, x,y,i);
        if(separated == true) sprite[i]=new Sprite(size, x,
y,c,ch,vx,vy);
        else i--;
      }
   }

private boolean checkSeparation(float size, float x, float y, int i){
      double sepX, sepY, sep;
      for(int index=0; index<i; index++){
        sepX = Math.abs(x-sprite[index].x);
        sepY = Math.abs(y-sprite[index].y);
        sep=Math.sqrt(sepX*sepX + sepY*sepY);
        if (sep<size) return false;
      }
      return true;
}
```

An interesting feature of this approach is that although we create these new sprites in a method each of them is visible to all of ShapeView. This is because when an object is modified or created in Java it is the original version that is changed in memory so this is what is then seen by all other parts of the program. This is not true of simple variables, which are copied to a method and only the copies are changed - then deleted after the method finishes. The original is left unchanged so unless a return statement is used to return a value, the new value is lost.

The setup() method needs copies of w, h and size to set up the sprites so these variables are now declared as instance variables instead of in the constructor as before. It uses its own versions of x, y, vx and vy which then become the properties of the sprite objects so, again, they are not lost to the rest of the program..

We create the random values of x and y as before using size, w and h to keep them all within the screen boundaries.

```
x= (float)(size/2+Math.random()*(w-size));
y= (float)(size/2+Math.random()*(h-size));
```

For vx and vy we have a different problem. We want random speeds in random directions but no zero values which would leave the ball stationary. So we have a complicated algorithm that generates a random number from 0 to the value of vxMax or vyMax, which are both 4 in this case. Adding 1 then gives the resulting random value in the range 1 to 3.

But we still have a problem since all the random numbers are positive so all the balls would start off all moving to the right and downwards. To get half of them going in the opposite direction we create another random number in the range -0.5 to 0.5 and assign it to the direction variable. If direction gets a negative result we reverse the direction of vx or vy. It is a bit complicated, but it works.

```
vx=(float) Math.random()*vx+1;// number from 1 to vx+1
direction= Math.random()-0.5;
if(direction<0)vx=-vx;      //   to get some negative directions
vy=(float) Math.random()*vy+1;
direction= Math.random()-0.5;
if(direction<0)vy=-vy;
```

The Timer Code

We can apply our new knowledge of timing threads by adding the standard code,

```
    timer = new Timer();
    timer.schedule(new TimerTask(){
       public void run(){
          runOnUiThread(new Runnable(){
            @Override
             public void run() {
               move();
               invalidate(); //after they have all moved
            }
          });
        }
      },0,20);
    }
```

This just runs a method move() every 20 milliseconds followed by a call to invalidate() to run the view's onDraw() method and refresh the display.

Moving the Sprite

This is a very simple method but it contains calls to two other methods that are far from simple. In fact, the only problem with this method is where to put it. We have to decide if it should be a ShapeView method or a Sprite method.

These design decisions keep cropping up. It is often not clear which is the best approach until you have tried one and found that it works or does not work. The general strategy is to use the "expert" class, that is, the class that has the required knowledge to do the job without having to import data from other classes.

In this case we need to use the width and height of the screen as well as the size of the sprite in order to test for collisions with the edges of the screen. We also need to know about all the sprites as well as the one we are moving so that we can test for collisions between sprites. We could carry out these operations in the Sprite class but it is logically simpler to do it in ShapeView.

So the code is

```
private void move(){
   for(int i=0;i<sprite.length;i++){
      sprite[i].x+=sprite[i].vx;
      sprite[i].y+=sprite[i].vy;
      reflect(i);
      bounce(i);
   }
}
```

This uses a for loop to move all the sprites in turn, or, to be more precise, to change their position coordinates so that they will be moved in the next call to onDraw().

In the loop, the x and y variables of each sprite are incremented by their own values of vx and vy. Then there are calls to reflect() and bounce(). The first method deals with the sprite bouncing of the sides of the screen and the second deals with possible bounces off other sprites. Both are delegated to helper methods to keep the logic as clear as possible.

The Reflect() Method

When a sprite comes within a radius of a wall it should perform a reflect action. Because our x and y position coordinates for the sprite refer to its center point, it should reflect off a side when it comes within half of its size parameter. If it is circular, this would be its radius. We could just reverse the value of vx or vy to produce reflection but it is more accurate to deal with each side in turn.

So, if the sprite is within size/2 of the left screen edge we immediately set its position to exactly size/2 to get it back on-screen, then reverse the x-speed, vx, to make it travel in the opposite direction. Of course, this does not change the y-speed, yx, so the net result is a reflection process like light off a mirror, or a ball off a wall.

We then repeat the operation for the other side. If the sprite is more than a distance, w-size/2 of the edge, it is moved back to that position and the x-direction reversed.

Then we do the same for the y direction to get reflection from the top and bottom edges of the screen and the full code is

```
private void reflect(int i){
    if(sprite[i].x<size/2){
        sprite[i].x=size/2;
        sprite[i].vx=-sprite[i].vx;
    }
    if(sprite[i].x>w-size/2){
        sprite[i].x=w-size/2;
        sprite[i].vx=-sprite[i].vx;
    }
    if(sprite[i].y<size/2){
        sprite[i].y=size/2;
        sprite[i].vy=-sprite[i].vy;
    }
    if(sprite[i].y>h-size/2){
        sprite[i].y=h-size/2;
        sprite[i].vy=-sprite[i].vy;
    }
}
```

You might have expected a series of if-else statements. We used straight if statement to allow for sprites that bounce off a corner of the screen, so we can't exclude the other possibilities if it hits both edges.

The Bounce() Method

It is a notoriously difficult calculation to derive an algorithm for two balls bouncing off each other. It certainly involves more math and physics expertise than most novice programmers might have. In any case, we are not trying to simulate real collisions, but only to stop the sprites running through each other.

So we can use a simple algorithm which just switches the speeds of two sprites when they collide. This makes them rebound in opposite directions, which is realistic enough.

However, if the math and physics are easy, the programming is not. First, to swap the speed values, in fact to swap anything, we need a temporary variable to store one value while it is being replaced by the other, so we introduce tempvx and tempvy for this puspose. Then we need three double precision variables, sep, sepX and sepY to calculate the separation of colliding sprites.

We run through a for loop to check the separation of each j-indexed sprite from the current i-indexed sprite is greater than the size of a sprite. If it is not, they are touching and should bounce. We have to be careful not to compare our j sprite with itself and we would prefer not to do each sprite twice, so we start the i-loop at i=j, then as j increases from zero we only test the remaining pairs. The code is

```
private void bounce(int i){
    float tempvx, tempvy;
    double sep, sepX, sepY;
    for(int j=i+1; j<sprite.length; j++){
        sepX = Math.abs(sprite[i].x-sprite[j].x);
        sepY = Math.abs(sprite[i].y-sprite[j].y);
        sep=Math.sqrt(sepX*sepX + sepY*sepY);
        if(sep<=size) {
            tempvx=sprite[i].vx;
            tempvy=sprite[i].vy;
            sprite[i].vx=sprite[j].vx;
            sprite[i].vy=sprite[j].vy;
```

```
            sprite[j].vx=tempvx;
            sprite[j].vy=tempvy;
            sprite[i].x+=sprite[i].vx;
            sprite[i].y+=sprite[i].vy;
            sprite[j].x+=sprite[j].vx;
            sprite[j].y+=sprite[j].vy;
        }
    }
}
```

Then we calculate sepX as the absolute value (positive value) of the distance between the x and the x coordinate of the current j sprite and each i-sprite. We do the same for sepY then use these to calculate the separation. For this we use the fact that the square of the length of the hypotenuse of a triangle is equal to the sum of the squares of the other two sides. So sep is given by

sep=Math.sqrt(sepX*sepX + sepY*sepY);

Then if this is less than the size of a sprite, they are touching.

In that case, we have to decide what to do and our solution is to swap speeds. So in the remaining code we copy the vx and vy into the temporary variables, then copy the vx and vy values of the j-sprite into the i-sprite and complete the switch by copying the temporary values into the j-sprite. Then we increment the x and y values of both sprites to move them away from the scene.

The onDraw() Method

There are no real changes here. The code just cycles through the sprite array and uses the sprite draw() method to draw the sprite.

```
public void onDraw(Canvas canvas){
    for(int i=0;i<sprite.length;i++){
```

```
    sprite[i].draw(canvas);
    }
}
```

The Result

The result of running the Movers app is to display the 16 ball objects on the device screen. They start off in random positions and moving in random directions. They bounce off the sides of the screen and each other exactly as intended. A still screen capture is provided in Figure 1 and the animation can be seen by downloading the free Movers app from the Google Play Store.

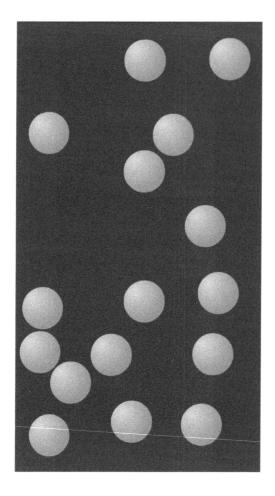

Figure 1. A still screenshot of the Movers app.

And the complete activity code is

```
package com.androidjavaapps.movers;

import android.os.*;
import android.app.*;
import android.view.*;
import android.content.*;
import android.graphics.*;
```

```java
import java.util.*;

public class MainActivity extends Activity {

    ShapeView shapeView;

    @Override
    protected void onCreate(Bundle savedInstanceState) {
        super.onCreate(savedInstanceState);
        this.requestWindowFeature(Window.FEATURE_NO_TITLE);
        getWindow().setFlags(WindowManager.LayoutParams.
          FLAG_FULLSCREEN,
WindowManager.LayoutParams.FLAG_FULLSCREEN);
        shapeView=new ShapeView(this);
        setContentView(shapeView);
    }

    public class ShapeView extends View{
        Sprite[] sprite;
        Timer timer;
        TimerTask timerTask;
        float w, h, size;

        public ShapeView(Context context){
            super(context);
            w=getResources().getDisplayMetrics().widthPixels;
            h=getResources().getDisplayMetrics().heightPixels;
            int n=6;
            if (w<h) size=w/n;
            else size= h/n;
            int c=Color.rgb(180,120,50);
            int ch=Color.rgb(200,200,200);
            int background=Color.rgb(40, 50, 60);
            setBackgroundColor(background);
```

```
        int elements=16;
        sprite = new Sprite[elements];
        setup(c, ch);

        timer = new Timer();
        timer.schedule(new TimerTask(){
          public void run(){
            runOnUiThread(new Runnable(){
              @Override
              public void run() {
                move();
                invalidate(); //after they have all moved
              }
            });
          }
        },0,20);
      }

  public void setup(int c, int ch){
      boolean separated=true;
      double direction;
      float x, y, vx, vy, vxMax=4, vyMax=4;
      for (int i=0; i<sprite.length; i++){
        x= (float)(size/2+Math.random()*(w-size));
        y=(float)(size/2+Math.random()*(h-size));
        vx=(float) Math.random()*vxMax+1;
        direction= Math.random()-0.5;
        if(direction<0)vx=-vx; // to get negative directions
        vy=(float) Math.random()*vyMax+1;
        direction= Math.random()-0.5;
        if(direction<0)vy=-vy;
        separated = checkSeparation(size, x,y,i);
         if(separated == true) sprite[i]=new Sprite(size, x,
y,c,ch,vx,vy);
```

```
      else i--;
    }
  }

  private void move() {
    for(int i=0;i<sprite.length;i++){
      sprite[i].x+=sprite[i].vx;
      sprite[i].y+=sprite[i].vy;
      reflect(i);
      bounce(i);
    }
  }

  private boolean checkSeparation(float size, float x, float y, int i ){
    float sepX, sepY;
    for(int j=0; j<i; j++){
      sepX=Math.abs(x-sprite[j].x);
      sepY=Math.abs(y-sprite[j].y);
      if(sepX<size && sepY<size) return false;
    }
    return true;
  }

  public void onDraw(Canvas canvas) {
    for (int i = 0; i < sprite.length; i++) {
      sprite[i].draw(canvas);
    }
  }

  private void reflect(int i) {
    if (sprite[i].x < size / 2) {
      sprite[i].x = size / 2;
      sprite[i].vx = -sprite[i].vx;
    }
```

```
    if (sprite[i].x > w - size / 2) {
      sprite[i].x = w - size / 2;
      sprite[i].vx = -sprite[i].vx;
    }
    if (sprite[i].y < size / 2) {
      sprite[i].y = size / 2;
      sprite[i].vy = -sprite[i].vy;
    }
    if (sprite[i].y > h - size / 2) {
      sprite[i].y = h - size / 2;
      sprite[i].vy = -sprite[i].vy;
    }
  }

  private void bounce(int i){
      float tempvx, tempvy;
      double sep, sepX, sepY;
      for(int j=i+1; j<sprite.length; j++){
        sepX = Math.abs(sprite[i].x-sprite[j].x);
        sepY = Math.abs(sprite[i].y-sprite[j].y);
        sep=Math.sqrt(sepX*sepX + sepY*sepY);
        if(sep<=size) {
          tempvx=sprite[i].vx;
          tempvy=sprite[i].vy;
          sprite[i].vx=sprite[j].vx;
          sprite[i].vy=sprite[j].vy;
          sprite[j].vx=tempvx;
          sprite[j].vy=tempvy;
          sprite[i].x+=sprite[i].vx;
          sprite[i].y+=sprite[i].vy;
          sprite[j].x+=sprite[j].vx;
          sprite[j].y+=sprite[j].vy;
        }
      }
```

```
    }
  }
}
```

What Next

What you should do now is extend Movers to create your own version. You can, of course, publish this as your own work but you should remember to change the domain name to your own registered domain.

10. Animation

The Aim

The aim is now to add another feature to our app by animating the sprite. In addition to moving around the screen it will be able to change its shape in order to simulate some action such as walking or running. This is described as animation and usually accomplished by displaying a series of image frames, like a movie. So it is called frame animation

The effect is usually created by switching quickly between fixed images that are imported into the app. These may be ordinary image files often held as a complete collection in a single picture file called a spritesheet. This has a number of frames, each a separate image of a single still shot of the animation. These can be produced outside of Android with a separate graphics package and imported into the app resources. The app then cycles through these frames to simulate the animation effect.

However, we are trying to do everything in Java so we will not use the industry standard approach. Instead we will draw our successive frames in Java and display them in sequence.

Animated Sprites

We have to replace our single sprite drawing with a series of drawings that are going to be displayed in turn. The series will be repeated indefinitely to create the animation. We have to regulate the time between these repeats and ideally start at a different point in the cycle for each animated object – unless of course we want them all to move precisely in sync.

All the frames can be separate parts of the sprite's draw() method and selected by an index that is periodically incremented from the start position.

The good news is that there are very few modifications required in the ShapeView class. We just have to choose new colors for the variables c and ch and add a single statement to the move() method to increment the sprite frame each time it is moved.

```
private void move(){
    for(int i=0;i<sprite.length;i++){
        sprite[i].count++;   // increment sprite frame
        sprite[i].x+=sprite[i].vx;
        sprite[i].y+=sprite[i].vy;
        reflect(i);
        bounce(i);
    }
}
```

So we start a new project with the name Shakers and the appropriate package name and the MainActivity file can be copied directly from the Movers app.

The Sprite Class

The Sprite class does not have to be modified very much from the previous version to produce an animated sprite. We can describe the changes in two halves. First for the attributes and the constructor then for the draw() method.

```
package com.androidjavaapps.shakers;

import android.graphics.*;

public class Sprite {
    float size, x, y, vx, vy;
    float r, u;
    int c, ch;
    Paint paint =new Paint(Paint.ANTI_ALIAS_FLAG);
    float w,h;
    Path path;
    int count, start, frame, frames, rate;

public Sprite(float size, float x, float y, int c, int ch, float vx, float vy){
    this.size=size;
    this.x=x;
    this.y=y;
    r=size/2;
    u=size/80;
    this.c=c;
    this.ch=ch;
    this.vx=vx;
    this.vy=vy;
    count=0;
    frames=8;
    rate=10;     // the number of movements per frame
    start=(int) (Math.random()*frames);
    path=new Path();
}
```

The attributes need five additional variables, count, start, frame, frames and rate, all ints. These are then initialized in the constructor, as usual. The count variable is the number of times the sprite has been drawn and is incremented in the ShapeView object. The start variable is the starting frame of the sprite which will be assigned some random value. The frame variable is the frame number that is to be drawn. The frames variable represents the total number of frames used, in this case, 8, and the rate is the speed at which they are drawn. This is defined as the number of screen refreshes per frame, in this case 10. So it means that for every 10 moves of the sprite there is a single animation change. We found this value by trial and error. Any faster and the animation is too quick. Any slower and it is not smooth enough.

The start frame number for each sprite instance is determined by a random number generator,

start=(int) (Math.*random*()*frames);

This assigns the starting frame a random number of 0 to 7 so that the sprite animations start at different points in the frame cycle. If you want them to start in sync then you might assign the start frame to 0 for all sprites instances.

The draw() Method

We have to decide what to draw that can be animated by code. So we will draw a round face with large eyes and a mouth. We will make the eyes roll by drawing them at different positions in successive frames. So the method starts by drawing a circle with the fill color, c, transferred from ShapeView. This is the face. Then we add two more circles for the whites of the eyes and then the animation in a set of 8 frames selected by a new decision structure called a switch – case structure.

```java
public void draw(Canvas canvas){
   paint.setStyle(Paint.Style.FILL);
    // draw round face
    paint.setColor(c);
    canvas.drawCircle(x, y, 40*u, paint);
    //draw two circles for whites of eyes
    paint.setColor(Color.rgb(200, 200, 200));
    canvas.drawCircle(x-17*u, y-6*u, 14*u, paint);
    canvas.drawCircle(x+17*u, y-6*u, 14*u, paint);
    //draw blue pupils at same points
    paint.setColor(Color.rgb(0, 100, 200));
    frame=(start + count/rate)%frames;
    switch (frame){
    case 0:
       canvas.drawCircle(x-17*u, y-13*u, 7*u, paint);
       canvas.drawCircle(x+17*u, y-13*u, 7*u, paint);//up
       break;
    case 1:
       canvas.drawCircle(x-14*u, y-10*u, 7*u, paint);
       canvas.drawCircle(x+20*u, y-10*u, 7*u, paint);
       break;
    case 2:
       canvas.drawCircle(x-10*u, y-6*u, 7*u, paint);
       canvas.drawCircle(x+24*u, y-6*u, 7*u, paint);//right
       break;
    case 3:
       canvas.drawCircle(x-14*u, y-5*u, 7*u, paint);
       canvas.drawCircle(x+20*u, y-5*u, 7*u, paint);
       break;
    case 4:
       canvas.drawCircle(x-17*u, y-4*u, 7*u, paint);
       canvas.drawCircle(x+17*u, y-4*u, 7*u, paint);//straight
       break;
    case 5:
       canvas.drawCircle(x-20*u, y-5*u, 7*u, paint);
       canvas.drawCircle(x+14*u, y-5*u, 7*u, paint);
       break;
    case 6:
```

```
         canvas.drawCircle(x-24*u, y-6*u, 7*u, paint);
         canvas.drawCircle(x+10*u, y-6*u, 7*u, paint);//left
         break;
      case 7:
         canvas.drawCircle(x-20*u, y-10*u, 7*u, paint);
         canvas.drawCircle(x+14*u, y-10*u, 7*u, paint);
         break;
      default:
         break;
      }
      // draw the mouth
      path.reset();
      path.moveTo(x-24*u, y+16*u);
      path.lineTo(x-12*u, y+18*u);
      path.lineTo(x,y+20*u);
      path.lineTo(x+12*u, y+18*u);
      path.lineTo(x+24*u, y+16*u);
      path.lineTo(x+10*u,y+24*u);
      path.lineTo(x,y+26*u);
      path.lineTo(x-10*u,y+24*u);
      path.close();
      paint.setColor(ch);
      canvas.drawPath(path, paint);
   }

} // end of class
```

The switch – case Structure

The switch – case structure starts with a

switch() {

that is just like a method definition. However, in this case the contents of the brackets are a single conditional expression. The expression must be one that can be evaluated to a set of discrete values and these are listed in the following code as case options. So if the conditional expression evaluates to the first case value the associated code is executed. And so on down the other case values to the last one which is a default case that sweeps up any values that have been missed.

In this example the conditional expression is simply

```
switch (frame){
```

So it switches to the drawing code for each of the 8 frames depending on the current value of frame. This is calculated in the preceding statements,

```
count=count%(rate*frames);
frame=(start+count/rate)%frames;
```

We remember that the draw() method is called every time the sprite moves and at the same time the value of count is incremented in the view object. So the value of count would increase continually and well beyond the number of frames available. We would like it to count to a maximum required to give us a frame value in the range of 0 to 7. Since there are 10 counts per frame this means we have to restart the count at 0 each time it hits 80 counts. This is the value of rate*frames.

We can do this by using the modulus operator, %. This calculates the remainder after dividing count by rate*frames to give us the restarted value of count.

Then we have to calculate the current frame for each sprite. To do this we divide the count by the rate to get the number of frames to be incremented and add this to the start frame for the sprite object. The result will be some number between 0 and 15 for start values of 0 to 7, so we have to use the modulus operator again to get the remainder of this value after dividing by the number of frames. So now we have a correct frame number for each sprite.

In this example, when the switch expression evaluates to 0, we run the first frame with

```
case 0:
   canvas.drawCircle(x-17*u, y-13*u, 7*u, paint);
   canvas.drawCircle(x+17*u, y-13*u, 7*u, paint);    //up
   break;
```

This draws two circles to represent the eyes of the face sprite pointing upwards. Then it uses a break; statement to break out of the switch – case loop otherwise the program would just go on to the next case statement

The next case is

```
case 1:
   canvas.drawCircle(x-14*u, y-10*u, 7*u, paint);
   canvas.drawCircle(x+20*u, y-10*u, 7*u, paint);
   break;
```

to draw the eyes moved slightly down and to the right.

Then the remaining 6 cases draw the eyes at incremented coordinates that move them in a roll round to the left and back up again. The draw() method then ends by using a path object to draw a mouth shape. This path is created in the constructor and reset in each animation otherwise it would continue to draw the original path.

The Outcome

The result of this program is illustrated in the screenshot of Figure 1 and the actual animation can be seen by downloading the free Shakers app from the Play Store.

Figure 1. A snapshot of the Shakers app in action.

The Final Code

With these modifications, the complete code for the activity is

package com.androidjavaapps.shakers;

import android.os.*;
import android.app.*;
import android.view.*;
import android.content.*;
import android.graphics.*;
import java.util.*;

public class MainActivity extends Activity {

   ShapeView shapeView;

   @Override
   protected void onCreate(Bundle savedInstanceState) {
     super.onCreate(savedInstanceState);
     this.requestWindowFeature(Window.FEATURE_NO_TITLE);
     getWindow().setFlags(WindowManager.LayoutParams.
       FLAG_FULLSCREEN,
WindowManager.LayoutParams.FLAG_FULLSCREEN);
     shapeView=new ShapeView(this);
     setContentView(shapeView);
   }

   public class ShapeView extends View{
     Sprite[] sprite;
     Timer timer;
     TimerTask timerTask;
     float w, h, size;

```
public ShapeView(Context context){
    super(context);
    w=getResources().getDisplayMetrics().widthPixels;
    h=getResources().getDisplayMetrics().heightPixels;
    int n=6;
    if (w<h) size=w/n;
    else size= h/n;
    int c=Color.rgb(180,120,50);
    int ch=Color.rgb(200,200,200);
    int background=Color.rgb(40, 50, 60);
    setBackgroundColor(background);
    int elements=16;
    sprite = new Sprite[elements];
    setup(c, ch);

    timer = new Timer();
    timer.schedule(new TimerTask(){
        public void run(){
            runOnUiThread(new Runnable(){
                @Override
                public void run() {
                    move();
                    invalidate(); //after they have all moved
                }
            });
        }
    },0,20);
}

public void setup(int c, int ch){
    boolean separated=true;
    double direction;
    float x, y, vx, vy, vxMax=4, vyMax=4;
```

```
        for (int i=0; i<sprite.length; i++){
            x= (float)(size/2+Math.random()*(w-size));
            y=(float)(size/2+Math.random()*(h-size));
            vx=(float) Math.random()*vxMax+1;
            direction= Math.random()-0.5;
            if(direction<0)vx=-vx; // to get negative directions
            vy=(float) Math.random()*vyMax+1;
            direction= Math.random()-0.5;
            if(direction<0)vy=-vy;
            separated = checkSeparation(size, x,y,i);
            if(separated == true) sprite[i]=new Sprite(size, x,
y,c,ch,vx,vy);
            else i--;
        }
    }

    private void move(){
        for(int i=0;i<sprite.length;i++){
            sprite[i].count++;   // increment sprite frame
            sprite[i].x+=sprite[i].vx;
            sprite[i].y+=sprite[i].vy;
            reflect(i);
            bounce(i);
        }
    }

    private boolean checkSeparation(float size, float x, float y, int i
){
        float sepX, sepY;
        for(int j=0; j<i; j++){
            sepX=Math.abs(x-sprite[j].x);
            sepY=Math.abs(y-sprite[j].y);
            if(sepX<size && sepY<size) return false;
        }
```

```java
    return true;
}

public void onDraw(Canvas canvas) {
    for (int i = 0; i < sprite.length; i++) {
        sprite[i].draw(canvas);
    }
}

private void reflect(int i) {
    if (sprite[i].x < size / 2) {
        sprite[i].x = size / 2;
        sprite[i].vx = -sprite[i].vx;
    }
    if (sprite[i].x > w - size / 2) {
        sprite[i].x = w - size / 2;
        sprite[i].vx = -sprite[i].vx;
    }
    if (sprite[i].y < size / 2) {
        sprite[i].y = size / 2;
        sprite[i].vy = -sprite[i].vy;
    }
    if (sprite[i].y > h - size / 2) {
        sprite[i].y = h - size / 2;
        sprite[i].vy = -sprite[i].vy;
    }
}

private void bounce(int i) {
    float tempvx, tempvy;
    double sep, sepX, sepY;
    for(int j=i+1; j<sprite.length; j++) {
        sepX = Math.abs(sprite[i].x-sprite[j].x);
        sepY = Math.abs(sprite[i].y-sprite[j].y);
```

```
            sep=Math.sqrt(sepX*sepX + sepY*sepY);
            if(sep<=size) {
                tempvx=sprite[i].vx;
                tempvy=sprite[i].vy;
                sprite[i].vx=sprite[j].vx;
                sprite[i].vy=sprite[j].vy;
                sprite[j].vx=tempvx;
                sprite[j].vy=tempvy;
                sprite[i].x+=sprite[i].vx;
                sprite[i].y+=sprite[i].vy;
                sprite[j].x+=sprite[j].vx;
                sprite[j].y+=sprite[j].vy;
            }
        }
    }
}
```

Color Animation

Kinetic art is a form of art that includes motion and animation. It is especially prominent as a form of computer art for obvious reasons. We can publish our Shakers app as kinetic art or upgrade it a little to make it more interesting. We will do this by adapting Shakers to form a new app called Kinetic.

One way to develop the animation further is to change the colors of the sprites in some way. We have been using two color variables, c and ch, in our programs without much justification other than creating gradients. The only reason for using variables transferred from the view class to the sprite is to be able to change them in the view. Otherwise all the sprites could have the same colors as, indeed, they have done so far.

So we could experiment with changing colors as well as animation. One way to do this is to use the ShapeView constructor to select starting colors and then use the move() method to change them in a programmed way. We can revise the Shakers code to change the sprite color depending on its position on the screen. For example, if we formulate the red component of the color palette to

255*(h-y)/h

It will give a maximum value of 255 for y = 0, that is at the top of the screen and this value will decrease gradually to 0 at the bottom of the screen, where y = h.

We can do the converse with the blue component with

255*y/h

Which will increase from 0 at the top of the screen to 255 at the bottom where y = h.

Then we can add a green formula to do the same across the screen and we have a color formula

c=Color.*rgb*((int)(255*(h-y)/h), (int)(255*x/w), (int)(255*y/h));

The int casts are required to cast the float position values to the ints required by the color variables.

We have to use this in the setup() method and the move() method so we declare the color variables in the attributes to make them visible to both.

Then the setup() and move() methods become

```
public void setup() {
    boolean separated=true;
    double direction;
    float x, y, vx, vy, vxMax=4, vyMax=4;
    for (int i=0; i<sprite.length; i++) {
        x= (float)(size/2+Math.random()*(w-size));
        y=(float)(size/2+Math.random()*(h-size));
        vx=(float) Math.random()*vxMax+1;
        direction= Math.random()-0.5;
        if(direction<0)vx=-vx;
        vy=(float) Math.random()*vyMax+1;
        direction= Math.random()-0.5;
        if(direction<0)vy=-vy;
        separated = checkSeparation(size, x,y,i);
        if(separated == true) {
            c=Color.rgb((int)(250*(h-y)/h), (int)(250*(w-x)/w),
int)(250*y/h));      // new color formula
            sprite[i]=new Sprite(size, x, y,c,ch,vx,vy);
        }
        else i--;
    }
}

private void move() {
    for(int i=0;i<sprite.length;i++) {
        sprite[i].frame++;
        sprite[i].x+=sprite[i].vx;
        sprite[i].y+=sprite[i].vy;
        sprite[i].c=Color.rgb((int)(250*(w-sprite[i].x)/w), (int)(250*(h-
sprite[i].y)/h), (int)(250*(sprite[i].y)/h));  // new color
        reflect(i);
        bounce(i);
    }
}
```

So the final version of Kinetic is as illustrated by the screenshot in Figure 2.

Figure 2. The version of kinetic with color formula.

What Next

You can extend both the Shakers and Kinetic apps to make your own version and publish your own computer art.

11. Interaction

The Aim

This chapter is about interactive apps. It concentrates on the events that are created by user interactions that involve touching the screen. The aim is to create a set of screen objects that can be pushed about on the screen to form a picture. It is the basis for apps that allow the user to assemble pictures or drawings from a set of components.

The app can be extended from the previous Shakers app by removing the motion and animation properties and replacing them with interactive ones. Then of course, we will have to redesign the Sprite draw() method to get a set of drawing shapes. We will call it Pushers.

First, however, we have to spend some time developing the Java theory of events.

Events

Most modern apps are driven by events. These are mostly generated by user interactions with the Android device and mainly with the screen. The events we will consider here are the touch events.

An event is a message sent through the Android operating system to the app. It has a predefined Android name so that the programmer knows what to expect. It also has a number of methods designed to respond to the event and these too have predefined names and have to be programmed to deal with the event in some way.

The event message is created at some position on a View object. The object has to have an additional inheritance in the form of an event listener. The event listener is an interface which is, in effect, a class with no method implementations. It only has a name and some method names but the methods are blank and have to be coded, or implemented, by the programmer.

As we have seen, when a new class is defined it can inherit the entire code of a class. So ShapeView, for example, has been defined to inherit the View class. ShapeView objects are also View objects.

But the class can also inherit an interface and it does this by using the keyword, implements. This is because it implements the code of the interface methods. In Java, a new class can inherit only one existing class but it can implement several interfaces.

Each of the interface methods has a name that is fixed by Android so the programmer has to include these methods and provide code for them.

For example, a simple touch event is created when the user touches the screen of an Android device. This message is passed from the screen view by Android to the app where it is detected by an event listener interface called an OnTouchListener.

To detect the event, this interface must have been already added to the import list and to the View object being touched, by using the implements keyword in the class definition.

So we need another import,

import android.view.View.*;

and a modification to the ShapeView declaration

public class ShapeView extends View implements OnTouchListener

Then it must be set by the setOnTouchListener() method of the View object with the current view object as its argument.

setOnTouchListener(this);

Finally, the OnTouchListener interface has a method,

onTouch(View view, MotionEvent motionEvent)

which has to be programmed to respond to the touch event. It is sometimes described as a callback method since it calls back to the touch event itself. It has parameters provided by the event in the form of the view that has registered it and a MotionEvent object that contains further information about the event, such as its location on the view screen.

There are many event listeners available to the Android programmer but we need only mention a few of the interfaces here. They include,

- OnTouchListener – detects any touch events and calls onTouch().
- OnClickListener – detects single tap events (like mouse clicks) and calls onClick().
- OnLongClickListener – detects long touches and calls onLongClick().

- OnKeyListener – detects that a key has been pressed and calls onKeyPressed().

There are also some other events for moving touches, or swipes, and for multiple touches, such as pinching with two fingers. These are called gestures. We will not be using any of them in this book but it is a topic you may want to explore later.

Interactive Objects

We can demonstrate the use of touch events by adding event listeners to our previous app. We will convert all of our Sprites to interactive objects and call them Pieces. They will behave like the pieces used in board games, without the motion and the animation, but the ability to be dragged or pushed across the screen. We also want to have a set of different shaped pieces as in a board game, like chess.

We will call the app Pushers. It can be created in the usual way by copying the code of MainActivity from the Shakers app then editing the code, then copying and reprogramming the Sprite class.

But make sure you keep a copy of the original Shakers code because we will be going back to that to modify it for the next app. We will also want to reuse the Sprite class.

In the copy of MainActivity we can delete all the code involving the velocity parameters, vx and vy, and the direction variable from the setup() method. Then we delete the move(), reflect() and bounce() methods. Then we delete all the Timer code from the creation of the Timer object to the end of the run thread and the declarations of the Timer and TimerTask instance variables. The program should now run with the existing sprites but they should not move.

The MainActivity code should now be,

```
package com.androidjavaapps.pushers;

import android.os.*;
import android.app.*;
import android.view.*;
import android.content.*;
import android.graphics.*;
import java.utils.*;   // not required but keep for next app
import android.view.View.*;

public class MainActivity extends Activity {

    ShapeView shapeView;

    @Override
    protected void onCreate(Bundle savedInstanceState) {
        super.onCreate(savedInstanceState);
        this.requestWindowFeature(Window.FEATURE_NO_TITLE);
        getWindow().setFlags(WindowManager.LayoutParams.
            FLAG_FULLSCREEN,
WindowManager.LayoutParams.FLAG_FULLSCREEN);
        shapeView=new ShapeView(this);
        setContentView(shapeView);
    }

public class ShapeView extends View implements OnTouchListener{
    Piece[] piece;
    float w, h, size;
    int index=0, found=0;     // to find the touched sprite

    public ShapeView(Context context){
        super(context);
```

```
        w=getResources().getDisplayMetrics().widthPixels;
        h=getResources().getDisplayMetrics().heightPixels;
        int n=6;
        if (w<h) size=w/n;
        else size= h/n;
        int c=Color.rgb(180,120,50);
        int ch=Color.rgb(200,200,200);
        int background=Color.rgb(40, 50, 60);
        setBackgroundColor(background);
        int elements=16;
        piece = new Piece[elements];
        setup(c, ch);
        setOnTouchListener(this);
    }

  public void setup(int c, int ch){
        boolean separated=true;
        float x, y, vx, vy, vxMax=4, vyMax=4;
        for (int i=0; i<piece.length; i++){
            x= (float)(size/2+Math.random()*(w-size));
            y= (float)(size/2+Math.random()*(h-size));
            separated = checkSeparation(size, x,y,i);
            if(separated == true) piece[i]=new Piece(size, x, y,c,ch);
            else i--;
        }
    }

private boolean checkSeparation(float size, float x, float y, int i){
        double sepX, sepY, sep;
        for(int index=0; index<i; index++){
            sepX = Math.abs(x-sprite[index].x);
            sepY = Math.abs(y-sprite[index].y);
            sep=Math.sqrt(sepX*sepX + sepY*sepY);
            if (sep<size) return false;
        }
        return true;
}
```

```
public void onDraw(Canvas canvas){
    for(int i=0;i<piece.length;i++){
        piece[i].draw(canvas);
    }
}
}
}
```

Adding Events

Now we have to add the code that will allow the user to touch and drag the pieces on the screen. All of the code for this must be in the ShapeView class since we can only add the touch interfaces to a View. Clearly there is going to be a problem in knowing which of the pieces on the view is selected when the user touches it, but we will deal with that.

There are three modifications to be made to ShapeView,

- The code, implements OnTouchListener must be added to the class definition
- The android.view.View.* package should be added to the imports.
- The setOnTouchListener(this) call must be added to the ShapeView constructor.
- The onTouch() method must be programmed to find and move the sprite object.

The onTouch() Method

This is the difficult part. The method must have two parameters, a
View and a MotionEvent object and it must return a boolean value,
true or false. So the empty method is

```
public boolean onTouch(View view, MotionEvent event){
    return true;
}
```

The program will compile and run with this but, of course, it will not
respond to any touches. To achieve this result we have to do some
complicated coding.

The touch event has three useful actions represented by constant
class attributes of the MotionEvent class. These detect a touch down,
a touch move and a touch up action so we can use them to detect the
initial touch, the drag action and the end of the movement when the
finger is removed from the screen. The touch down action will let us
determine which, if any, object has been selected, the touch move
action will let us move the object and the touch up will let us end the
operation and forget the object.

We can decide which of these three separate events is taking place
with a switch case selection,

```
switch (event.getAction()){

case MotionEvent.ACTION_DOWN:
    break;

case MotionEvent.ACTION_MOVE:
    break;

case MotionEvent.ACTION_UP:
    break;
```

```
default:
   break;
}
```

Finding the Object

To find the object that has been touched we use the x and y positions
of the event and assign these values to local variables x and y. We will
use the same code for the move action so these are declared and
initialized before the switch case process. So we have

```
public boolean onTouch(View v, MotionEvent event){
    float px, py, pr, dx,dy;
    float x = event.getRawX();
    float y = event.getRawY();

    switch (event.getAction()){
```

We are also going to make life easy by using some local variables px,
py, pr, dx and dy. The px variable will replace the much longer code
piece[i].x, py will replace piece[i].y and pr will replace piece[i].r and
make our statements much shorter. The dx and dy will be explained
shortly.

After these declarations the code declares two floats, x and y, and
initializes them to the x and y attributes of the event object with the
methods, getRawX() and getRawY(). So each time the piece is
touched or moved the current position of the users finger on the
screen is provided by these variables, x and y.

In the first switch case option we iterate through all the pieces in the
array and measure its separation from the touch coordinates. If this is
less than the size of a piece the iteration ends before completing the
loop with a return statement to return a true value. If it finds no

touch it ends with a break and goes on to exit at the final return true statement.

```
switch (event.getAction()){

    case MotionEvent.ACTION_DOWN:
    for(int i=0;i<piece.length;i++){
        px=piece[i].x;
        py=piece[i].y;
        pr=size/2;
        if (x<px+pr&&x>px-pr&& y<py+pr&&y>py-pr){
            dx=px-x;
            dy=py-y;
            piece[i].x=x+dx;
            piece[i].y=y+dy;
            piece[i].dx=dx;
            piece[i].dy=dy;
            found=1;
            index=i;
            return true;
        }
    }
    break;
```

If the code does find a match then before exiting the loop it saves the value of i, the index value of the piece element that is found to be touched. This is saved in the instance variable, index, so that its value is not lost when another event is registered.

It also saves the x and y coordinates of the piece but first it adds increments dx and dy to these values. These are the exact differences between the x and y event coordinates and the piece[i] x and y positions. They are added to the piece position so that when it is moved it will always be the same distance from the touch event. So when the user touches then moves the piece it retains its relative position with regard to the finger position.

There is another piece instance variable used in this code, found. This is initialized to 0 meaning that no touching piece has been found. So when one is found it is set to 1. This means that if the next event is a move it will know that a piece has already been found and that its index is saved in the index variable. In other words, it will know which piece to move.

These new variables, index and found have to be declared outside the onTouch() method since it is called on each event. That is, the down and move events are quite separate events. So the index and found variables are declared in the ShapeView attributes.

Moving the Piece

The move event is completely separate from any other including the touch down so it has to check if a piece has been found. Then, if found > 0 it sets the piece index to index and its x and y coordinates to the event x and y plus the value of dx and dy saved for this piece.

```
case MotionEvent.ACTION_MOVE:
   if(found>0){
     piece[index].x=x+piece[index].dx;
     piece[index].y=y+piece[index].dy;
   }
   break;
```

Then if this event is followed by a succession of move events the x and y coordinates of the piece keep getting updated to the new position so the piece follows the moving finger across the screen

The movement is only terminated when the finger is lifted from the screen generating an ACTION_UP event. This resets found to 0 so that any further movement will have to find a sprite first.

```
case MotionEvent.ACTION_UP:
   found=0;
   break;
default:
```

```
}
invalidate();
  return true;
}
```

Finally the movement is completed by forcing a screen refresh with the invalidate() method.

One point to note about these event handling methods is that they return a boolean value. If it is true, the event has been successfully dealt with. If it is false, the event remains open for another listener to respond to it. The usual choice is true, as in the above code.

So the full code for the onTouch() method is

```
public boolean onTouch(View v, MotionEvent event){
    float px, py, pr, dx,dy;
    float x = event.getRawX();
    float y = event.getRawY();

    switch (event.getAction()){

    case MotionEvent.ACTION_DOWN:
      for(int i=0;i<piece.length;i++){
        px=piece[i].x;
        py=piece[i].y;
        pr=size/2;
         if (x<px+pr&&x>px-pr&& y<py+pr&&y>py-pr){
           dx=px-x;
           dy=py-y;
           piece[i].x=x+dx;
           piece[i].y=y+dy;
           piece[i].dx=dx;
           piece[i].dy=dy;
           found=1;
             index=i;
             return true;
        }
```

```
      }
      break;

   case MotionEvent.ACTION_MOVE:
      if(found>0){
         piece[index].x=x+piece[index].dx;
         piece[index].y=y+piece[index].dy;
      }
      break;

   case MotionEvent.ACTION_UP:
      found=0;
      break;

   default:
   }
   invalidate();
   return true;
}
```

The Piece Class

The program described so far produces a set of faces that can be dragged about the screen by touching one of them and moving the finger. However, there is not much point in dragging faces around the screen so we will complete the app by redesigning the Sprite class to form a new Piece class.

The aim is to display a set of geometrical shapes on the screen and allow the user to slide them into various positions in order to create a picture of some sort. In that case we need a piece that can have several shapes and, perhaps, colors, like the pieces of a board game or a jig-saw puzzle.

The Shakers sprite can be edited for this purpose. We can delete the count, start, frames and rate variables since we do not need them but we will keep the frame variable. This can be used to point to different shapes. The question is how we can select these frames. One way is to generate random numbers to do the job, with

frame=(int)(3*Math.*random*());

This generates an integer in the range 0 to less than 3 so we can have 3 frames to draw 3 shapes. We use a switch case selection where the first case 0 draws a red rectangle, the second case 1 draws a blue circle and the third case 2 draws a green triangle. We have fixed these colors in the piece and ignored the colors c and ch set in the View class so that we can develop this piece further and might need these options.

So the complete code for the Piece class is listed below and an illustration of the app output is shown in Figure 1.

```
package com.androidjavaapps.pushers;

import android.graphics.*;

public class Piece {

    float size, x, y, dx,dy;
    float r, u;
    int c=Color.GREEN, ch=Color.WHITE;
    Paint paint =new Paint(Paint.ANTI_ALIAS_FLAG);
    float w=400,h=800;
    Path path;
    int frame;

    public Piece(float size, float x, float y, int c, int ch){
        this.size=size;
        this.x=x;
        this.y=y;
```

```java
        r=size/2;
        u=size/80;
        this.c=c;
        this.ch=ch;
        dx=0;
        dy=0;
        frame=(int)(3*Math.random());
        path=new Path();
    }

public void draw(Canvas canvas){
    paint.setStyle(Paint.Style.FILL);
    switch (frame){
    case 0:      // rectangle
        paint.setColor(Color.rgb(250,50,50));
        canvas.drawRect(x-r,y-r,x+r,y+r, paint);
        break;
    case 1:      // circle
        paint.setColor(Color.rgb(50,50,250));
        canvas.drawCircle(x,y,r,paint);
        break;
    case 2:      // triangle
        path.reset();
        path.moveTo(x, y-r/2);
        path.lineTo(x+r,y+r);
        path.lineTo(x-r,y+r);
        path.close();
        paint.setColor(Color.rgb(50,250,50));
        canvas.drawPath(path, paint);
        break;
    default:
        break;
    }
  }
}
```

Figure 1. The output of the Players app.

Final Code

The complete code for the MainActivity is as follows:-

```
package com.androidjavaapps.pushers;

import android.os.*;
import android.app.*;
```

```java
import android.view.*;
import android.content.*;
import android.graphics.*;
import android.view.View.*;

public class MainActivity extends Activity {

ShapeView shapeView;

@Override
protected void onCreate(Bundle savedInstanceState) {
    super.onCreate(savedInstanceState);
    this.requestWindowFeature(Window.FEATURE_NO_TITLE);
    getWindow().setFlags(WindowManager.LayoutParams.
        FLAG_FULLSCREEN,
WindowManager.LayoutParams.FLAG_FULLSCREEN);
    shapeView=new ShapeView(this);
    setContentView(shapeView);
}

public class ShapeView extends View implements OnTouchListener{
    Piece[] piece;
    float w, h, size;
    int index=0, found=0;     // to find the touched sprite

    public ShapeView(Context context){
        super(context);
        w=getResources().getDisplayMetrics().widthPixels;
        h=getResources().getDisplayMetrics().heightPixels;
        int n=6;
        if (w<h) size=w/n;
        else size= h/n;
        int c=Color.rgb(180,120,50);
        int ch=Color.rgb(200,200,200);
```

```
    int background=Color.rgb(40, 50, 60);
    setBackgroundColor(background);
    int elements=16;
    piece = new Piece[elements];
    setup(c, ch);
    setOnTouchListener(this);
}

public void setup(int c, int ch){
    boolean separated=true;
    float x, y, vx, vy, vxMax=4, vyMax=4;
    for (int i=0; i<piece.length; i++){
        x= (float)(size/2+Math.random()*(w-size));
        y= (float)(size/2+Math.random()*(h-size));
        separated = checkSeparation(size, x,y,i);
        if(separated == true) piece[i]=new Piece(size, x, y,c,ch);
        else i--;
    }
}

private boolean checkSeparation(float size, float x, float y, int i){
    double sepX, sepY, sep;
    for(int index=0; index<i; index++){
        sepX = Math.abs(x-piece[index].x);
        sepY = Math.abs(y-piece[index].y);
        sep=Math.sqrt(sepX*sepX + sepY*sepY);
        if (sep<size) return false;
    }
    return true;
}

public void onDraw(Canvas canvas){
    for(int i=0;i<piece.length;i++){
        piece[i].draw(canvas);
```

```
    }
}

public boolean onTouch(View v, MotionEvent event){
    float px, py, pr, dx,dy;
    float x = event.getRawX();
    float y = event.getRawY();

    switch (event.getAction()){

        case MotionEvent.ACTION_DOWN:
            for(int i=0;i<piece.length;i++){
                px=piece[i].x;
                py=piece[i].y;
                pr=size/2;
                if (x<px+pr&&x>px-pr&& y<py+pr&&y>py-pr){
                    dx=px-x;
                    dy=py-y;
                    piece[i].x=x+dx;
                    piece[i].y=y+dy;
                    piece[i].dx=dx;
                    piece[i].dy=dy;
                    found=1;
                    index=i;
                    return true;
                }
            }
            break;

        case MotionEvent.ACTION_MOVE:
            if(found>0){
                piece[index].x=x+piece[index].dx;
                piece[index].y=y+piece[index].dy;
            }
```

```
            break;

        case MotionEvent.ACTION_UP:
            found=0;
            break;

        default:
    }
    invalidate();
    return true;
    }


    }
}
```

What Next

The most obvious extension of this app is to add more shapes and produce a drawing app where the user can assemble a picture by pushing shapes into place. You might also add more shapes and colors and perhaps a separate parking area for the shapes.

12. Action

The Aim

The aim is to produce the basic action of a ball game. It can be any game between two teams that compete for a single ball and the app simulates the action of a player from one team trying to get the ball from the opposing team. The game management code will be added in the next chapter.

The situation is a screen full of faces bouncing around like the sprites in the Shakers app. In fact, it is a straight copy of the sprites used in that app. The player is represented by a figure object which is another straight copy, this time of the face figure from the Picture app. The sprites represent members of the opposing team guarding a ball object randomly positioned on the screen. The aim is to get the ball without being caught by any of the opponents. If the player successfully collects the ball, by touching it, another one appears at a different position.

The idea is to collect as many balls as possible before being caught by the other team. The difficulty is in pushing the player around the screen while anticipating the movements of the opponents. This requires, and develops, concentration, good reflexes and anticipation, which are requisites for many ball games.

Since this is the basis of our final product, we will try to scale the main parameters so that a similar level of difficulty will be experienced on different devices. These include the size of the sprites and the number of sprites.

Design

A new project should be created in the usual way. We can call it Faces and start with the code from the main activity of the previous Shakers app. Then we create two new classes, Sprite and Figure. We can copy the Sprite code from Shakers and the Figure code from Picture and we are ready to start editing MainActivity. We can develop the app in easy stages, so in this, action stage we start with a number of sprites bouncing around the screen and we have to,

- Scale the sprite size and number to provide an appropriate level of difficulty for a range of devices.

- Add the Figure object to a starting position away from the initial positions of the sprites so that the player has time to think before moving.

- Add a new ball class to represent the ball and draw it at some random position on the screen.

- Add the onTouch() method to drag the Figure object. The method can be copied from the Pushers app and edited to refer to a single object.

- Add code to allow a figure to collect a ball then draw another one at a different position.

- Add a test for collision between the figure and a sprite and restart the game if it occurs.

Before we make these changes we can run the project to check that it produces the same output as the Shakers app. This is confirmation that the code has been copied correctly into the new app.

Scaling the App

We have been using the variable, n, to scale the app. This represents the number of sprites that would extend across the width of a device. However, there is a problem in that the sprites would be very small on small phone screens and too large on large tablet screens. What we would really like is to have a "finger" sized sprite on all of them. Then we would have fewer sprites on the phone and more sprites on the tablet but they would all be a convenient size for dragging.

The problem here is that these devices have various pixel densities, that is, the number of pixels per inch. Typically they range from less than 160 ppi to more than 300 ppi. So a fixed number of pixels would come out as different sizes on different devices. So we will set the size variable to half the value of the device's pixel density, which should be about half an inch.

This means abandoning the variable, n, and replacing the code lines

```
int n=6;
if (w<h) size=w/n;
else size= h/n;
int elements=(int) ((w*h)/(size*size*9));
```

with three new lines to get the pixel density from the DisplayMetrics and use that to set the size and elements variables. So the ShapeView constructor becomes,

```
public ShapeView(Context context){
    super(context);
    w=getResources().getDisplayMetrics().widthPixels;
    h=getResources().getDisplayMetrics().heightPixels;
    d = getResources().getDisplayMetrics().densityDpi;
    size=d/2;
    int elements=Math.round(w*h/(size*size*9));
    int background=Color.rgb(40, 50, 60);
    setBackgroundColor(background);
    sprite = new Sprite[elements];
}
```

We get the value of elements by simply dividing the area of the screen by 9 times the sprite area. If we imagine each sprite at the center of a 3 by 3 array, then it needs an area of size squared, times 9.

We also use the Math.round() method to get a more accurate conversion to the nearest integer value which might be very small for some screens in which case rounding down with a cast to int would be very inaccurate.

New Classes

Then we have to add two classes. The first addition is a Figure class which can be copied from the Picture app. In shapeView, we can use the color variable c for the sprite and the color variable ch for the figure so that they can be difference colors. In this example we have a pale blue sprite and an orange figure. The second color in both cases can be Color.WHITE and we can edit the eye colors to suit our preferences.

The other class is a new Ball class. The code for this can be copied from the Sprite class used in the Movers app, which is a ball object. However, we have to make a few modifications. First we need to change the name of the class and the constructor from Sprite to Ball. We also drop the ch color so the constructor now has only four parameters. We will have to adjust the call from MainActivity to match. Then we do not need the vx and vy parameters since it will not be moving. We will also make it smaller than the sprite so we can set the radius r to size/3 instead of size/2.

So the Ball class becomes,

```
public class Ball {
    float size, x, y;
    float r;
    int c, ch;
    RadialGradient radialGradient;
    Paint paint =new Paint(Paint.ANTI_ALIAS_FLAG);
    public Ball(float size, float x, float y, int c){
        this.size=size;
        this.x=x;
        this.y=y;
        this.c=c;
        r=size/3;
        ch=Color.WHITE;
    }

    public void draw(Canvas canvas){
        radialGradient = new RadialGradient(x-r/2,y-r/2,r*3/2,
ch,c,Shader.TileMode.CLAMP);
        paint.setShader(radialGradient);
```

```
    canvas.drawCircle(x, y, r, paint);
  }
}
```

We could test the app at this point but we need to edit the onDraw()
method to display all the objects, so the code becomes,

```
public void onDraw(Canvas canvas) {
    ball.draw(canvas);
    for (int i = 0; i < sprite.length; i++) {
      sprite[i].draw(canvas);
    }
    figure.draw(canvas);
}
```

We draw the ball first then the sprites on top of it, then the figure on
top of all of them.

Dragging the Figure

The next task is to make the figure draggable. This requires five
additions to ShapeView, namely

- The additional import of android.view.View.*
- The addition of implements OnTouchListener to the class
  definition
- The addition of a call to setOnTouchListener to the
  constructor
- The addition of the found variable to ShakeView attributes
- The coding of onTouch()

The onTouch() method can be copied from the Pushers app and edited. You have to remove all the for loops and replace piece[i] by figure to deal with only one object. Then you can also delete the references to dx and dy since we don't have to align the figure very accurately in this case.

So the onTouch() method becomes,

```
public boolean onTouch(View v, MotionEvent event){
    float px, py, pr;
    float x = event.getRawX();
    float y = event.getRawY();

    switch (event.getAction()){

        case MotionEvent.ACTION_DOWN:
            px=figure.x;
            py=figure.y;
            pr=size/2;
            if (x<px+pr&&x>px-pr&& y<py+pr&&y>py-pr){
                figure.x=x;
                figure.y=y;
                found=1;
                return true;
            }
            break;

        case MotionEvent.ACTION_MOVE:
            if(found>0){
                figure.x=x;
                figure.y=y;
            }
            break;
```

```
case MotionEvent.ACTION_UP:
    found=0;
    break;

default:
}
invalidate();
return true;
}
```

Now the figure can be dragged about on the screen.

Getting the Ball

We can collect the ball in a single new method, collect(). This must be run in each timer cycle so it is added to that code just after the move() method call.

```
private void collect() {
    if (Math.abs(ball.x - figure.x) < size / 2 &&
        Math.abs(ball.y - figure.y) < size / 2) {
        float x= (float)(size/2+Math.random()*(w-size));
        float y=(float)(size/2+Math.random()*(h-4*size));
        ball= new Ball(size, x, y, Color.RED);
    }
}
```

The method tests to see if the figure and the ball are within touching distance by simply comparing the x and y separations. If so, it creates a new red ball which replaces the previous one. Then onDraw() draws the new one.

Collisions

The only remaining problem is to deal with collisions between the figure and the faces. We already have a method, checkSeparation() that does this for the sprites but it would be complicated to adapt this. Instead we write a new method, checkCollision() which copies most of the code of checkSeparation(). We can call checkCollision() from the move() method for each sprite in turn.

This is quite straightforward but there is a problem in deciding what the app should do in the event of a collision. What we want to happen is that the app should restart. We can do this easily by calling setup().

So the full code for checkCollision() is

```
private void checkCollision(int j){
    float sepX, sepY;
    sepX=Math.abs(figure.x-sprite[j].x);
    sepY=Math.abs(figure.y-sprite[j].y);
    if(Math.sqrt(sepX*sepX+sepY*sepY)<size) {
        setup();
    }
}
```

This does the trick and resets the game to its starting setup although rather abruptly. We might want to add some some explanation for the user. Meanwhile the complete activity code is now as listed below and the output from the app is as illustrated in Figure 1.

```
package com.androidjavaapps.faces;
```

```
import android.os.*;
```

```
import android.app.*;
import android.view.*;
import android.content.*;
import android.graphics.*;
import java.util.*;
import android.view.View.*;

public class MainActivity extends Activity {

    ShapeView shapeView;

    @Override
    protected void onCreate(Bundle savedInstanceState) {
        super.onCreate(savedInstanceState);
        this.requestWindowFeature(Window.FEATURE_NO_TITLE);
        getWindow().setFlags(WindowManager.LayoutParams.
            FLAG_FULLSCREEN,
WindowManager.LayoutParams.FLAG_FULLSCREEN);
        shapeView=new ShapeView(this);
        setContentView(shapeView);
    }

    public class ShapeView extends View implements
OnTouchListener{
        Sprite[] sprite;
        Figure figure;
        Timer timer;
        float w, h, size;
        int c, ch;
        int found=0;
        Ball ball;

        public ShapeView(Context context){
            super(context);
```

```
w=getResources().getDisplayMetrics().widthPixels;
h=getResources().getDisplayMetrics().heightPixels;
d = getResources().getDisplayMetrics().densityDpi;
size=d/2;
int elements=Math.round(w*h/(size*size*9));
int background=Color.rgb(40, 50, 60);
setBackgroundColor(background);
sprite = new Sprite[elements];

setOnTouchListener(this);
setup();

timer = new Timer();
timer.schedule(new TimerTask(){
    public void run(){
        runOnUiThread(new Runnable(){
        @Override
        public void run() {
            move();
            collect();
            invalidate();
        }
        });
    }
},0,20);
}

public void setup(){
    boolean separated=true;
    double direction;
    float x, y, vx, vy, vxMax=4, vyMax=4;
    c=Color.rgb(100,150,250);
    ch=Color.rgb(200, 140, 80);
    figure = new Figure(size, w/2, h-size/2, ch, Color.WHITE);
```

```
for (int i=0; i<sprite.length; i++){
    x= (float)(size/2+Math.random()*(w-size));
    y=(float)(size/2+Math.random()*(h-4*size));
    vx=(float) Math.random()*vxMax+1;
    direction= Math.random()-0.5;
    if(direction<0)vx=-vx; // to get negative directions
    vy=(float) Math.random()*vyMax+1;
    direction= Math.random()-0.5;
    if(direction<0)vy=-vy;
    separated = checkSeparation(size, x,y,i);
    if(separated == true) sprite[i]=new Sprite(size, x,
y,c,Color.WHITE,vx,vy);
    else i--;
    }
    x= (float)(size/2+Math.random()*(w-size));
    y=(float)(size/2+Math.random()*(h-4*size));
    ball = new Ball(size, x, y,Color.RED);
}

private void move(){
    for(int i=0;i<sprite.length;i++){
        sprite[i].count++;   // increment sprite frame
        sprite[i].x+=sprite[i].vx;
        sprite[i].y+=sprite[i].vy;
        reflect(i);
        bounce(i);
        checkCollision(i);
    }
}

private void collect(){
    if (Math.abs(ball.x - figure.x) < size / 2 &&
        Math.abs(ball.y - figure.y) < size / 2 {
        float x= (float)(size/2+Math.random()*(w-size));
```

```
            float y=(float)(size/2+Math.random()*(h-4*size));
            ball= new Ball(size, x, y,Color.RED);
        }
    }

private boolean checkSeparation(float size, float x, float y, int i ){
    float sepX, sepY;
    for(int j=0; j<i; j++){
        sepX=Math.abs(x-sprite[j].x);
        sepY=Math.abs(y-sprite[j].y);
        if(sepX<size && sepY<size) return false;
    }
    return true;
}

    private void checkCollision(int j){
        float sepX, sepY;
        sepX=Math.abs(figure.x-sprite[j].x);
        sepY=Math.abs(figure.y-sprite[j].y);
        if(Math.sqrt(sepX*sepX+sepY*sepY)<size) {
            setup();
        }
    }

    public void onDraw(Canvas canvas) {
        ball.draw(canvas);
        for (int i = 0; i < sprite.length; i++) {
            sprite[i].draw(canvas);
        }
        figure.draw(canvas);
    }

    private void reflect(int i) {
        if (sprite[i].x < size / 2) {
```

```
      sprite[i].x = size / 2;
      sprite[i].vx = -sprite[i].vx;
   }
   if (sprite[i].x > w - size / 2) {
      sprite[i].x = w - size / 2;
      sprite[i].vx = -sprite[i].vx;
   }
   if (sprite[i].y < size/2) {
      sprite[i].y = size/2;
      sprite[i].vy = -sprite[i].vy;
   }
   if (sprite[i].y > h - size/2) {
      sprite[i].y = h - size/2;
      sprite[i].vy = -sprite[i].vy;
   }
}

private void bounce(int i){
   float tempvx, tempvy;
   double sep, sepX, sepY;
   for(int j=i+1; j<sprite.length; j++){
      sepX = Math.abs(sprite[i].x-sprite[j].x);
      sepY = Math.abs(sprite[i].y-sprite[j].y);
      sep=Math.sqrt(sepX*sepX + sepY*sepY);
      if(sep<=size) {
         tempvx=sprite[i].vx;
         tempvy=sprite[i].vy;
         sprite[i].vx=sprite[j].vx;
         sprite[i].vy=sprite[j].vy;
         sprite[j].vx=tempvx;
         sprite[j].vy=tempvy;
         sprite[i].x+=sprite[i].vx;
         sprite[i].y+=sprite[i].vy;
         sprite[j].x+=sprite[j].vx;
```

```
      sprite[j].y+=sprite[j].vy;
    }
  }
}

public boolean onTouch(View v, MotionEvent event){
  float px, py, pr;
  float x = event.getRawX();
  float y = event.getRawY();

  switch (event.getAction()){

    case MotionEvent.ACTION_DOWN:
        px=figure.x;
        py=figure.y;
        pr=size/2;
        if (x<px+pr&&x>px-pr&& y<py+pr&&y>py-pr){
          figure.x=x;
          figure.y=y;
          found=1;
          return true;
        }
      break;

    case MotionEvent.ACTION_MOVE:
      if(found>0){
        figure.x=x;
        figure.y=y;
      }
      break;

    case MotionEvent.ACTION_UP:
      found=0;
      break;
```

```
            default:
        }
        invalidate();
        return true;
    }
  }
}
```

Figure 1. The final action for the Faces app.

What Next

You can extend the game in many ways, for example, by redesigning the objects, changing their numbers and sizes and so on. A little experimentation with different screen sizes would be useful.

And you can test the app for yourself by downloading the final version from the Play Store.

13. Game

Making a Game of It

We have all the action of the game but no scoring or any game management so these features have to be added to complete the app. However, we are going to make substantial additions to the code so it would be a good idea to start a new project for our final product. It will be based on the Faces action app, which some would call the game engine, so we will extend that.

You should create a new project, which we will call BallGetter, then add three classes, Sprite, Figure and Ball. Then you should copy the code from the MainActivity of Faces to the new MainActivity and the code from the three classes, Sprite, Figure and Ball to the same classes in the new app. So our starting point is BallGetter which does exactly the same as Faces.

The first addition we require is an introductory screen with the game title and some instructions. It should also display the current score and the best score in the current session. The player should be able to navigate from this screen to the action screen where points are scored when balls are collected. Then, if the player collides with a sprite, they are returned to the introductory screen where the current and best scores are displayed. They can repeat the game play process as often as they want to.

MainActivity

The introductory screen can be implemented as an additional View. We can call this GameView and, like ShapeView it can be an inner class with full access to all the instance variables of the activity. This will make it easy to share data, such as the current score and the best score, between the two views.

So we have to declare two view objects in the activity attributes, gameView and shapeView, and use setContentView(gameView) to start the app. We also need two global int variables, score and best to store the current score and the best score. All of these variables can be initialized in the onCreate() method so the initial code is,

```
package com.androidjavaapps.runner;

import android.os.*;
import android.app.*;
import android.view.*;
import android.content.*;
import android.graphics.*;
import java.util.*;
import android.view.View.*;

public class MainActivity extends Activity {

    ShapeView shapeView;
    GameView gameView;
    int score=0, best=0;

    @Override
    protected void onCreate(Bundle savedInstanceState) {
        super.onCreate(savedInstanceState);
        this.requestWindowFeature(Window.FEATURE_NO_TITLE);
```

```
getWindow().setFlags(WindowManager.LayoutParams.
    FLAG_FULLSCREEN,
WindowManager.LayoutParams.FLAG_FULLSCREEN);
    shapeView=new ShapeView(this);
    gameView=new GameView(this);
    setContentView(gameView);
    score=0;
    best=0;
}
```

The GameView Class

This class will have a set of instance variables as its attributes, a constructor to initialize these variables, an onDraw() method to draw the view and an onTouch() method to respond to user touches and switch to shapeView.

The instance variables are two floats to hold the screen width and height so that we can scale the display, two ints for the colors, c and ch, a Figure object which we will use to enhance the display, three string variables and a paint object to draw on the screen. We also implement the OnTouchListener so that we can listen for touch events. And we need a paint object to draw on the screen.

The initial code is

```
public class GameView extends View implements OnTouchListener{
    float w, h;
    int c, ch;
    Figure figure;
    String heading, message1, message2, message3;
    Paint paint;
```

But first we need some more Java theory to introduce the String variables that we will need for our introductory screen.

String Variables

Java has only two built-in classes. One is the Array class, which we have already covered, and the other is a String class. They can be created with the new keyword and a constructor as for other objects but because they are intrinsic to the language they also have a simpler process.

We have been declaring arrays with the constructor, as for example,

Figure [ ] figures = new Figure[20];

This approach is particularly suited to looping through an array of objects. If we are dealing with an array of numbers, there is a quicker way to do the initializing. This uses braces to contain the starting values, sometimes described as a literal format since it uses literal (or constant) values,

int [ ] scores = {25, 30, 23, 10, 40};

A String is a "string" of text characters so it is quite similar in its structure to an array and has many similar attributes and methods. A String can also be declared with a constructor but there is little point in doing so, since they are always made up of simple char variables. So we use the literal format.

In this case, we do not have to use the String keyword or anything like the square bracket used for arrays. But we do have to enclose the value in quotation marks which are the equivalent of the array braces.

For example, we might have,

myString = "This is a text string";

So, in the GameView attributes we have declared four strings, heading, message1, message2 and message3.

Finally, there is one very useful property of strings that we will need. This is the concatenation of strings and variables. It is frequently necessary to output a variable value along with a string value describing the output and we can do this with concatenation, that is joining the two values. Eseentially, we join strings and other numeric variables using the + operator. Since it cannot add strings it automatically casts the numbers to strings and joins them up.

So to display a string "The result of your calculation is " followed by the value of a variable, result, we use

"The result of you calculation is " + result.

Noting the blank space at the end of the string to separate it from the following number.

Then, if result currently has the value 123, the displayed string is

The result of your calculation is 123

Displaying Strings

There are two general approaches to adding text to an Android screen. One is to use widgets, such as TextView and EditText to hold text strings. These must be added to a subclass of the View class called a Layout and this can be done with Java or, more commonly, as an XML layout file. This is a powerful approach that allows the programmer to format the text and to get user text input. However, it is a more complicated procedure than is necessary for an introduction to Android Java so we will use the other approach.

The alternative to text widgets is to use graphical text output in a View display. This uses strings and does not easily format text. Nor does it get user input. But it is sufficient for our purposes and, in fact, better in some respects since it can position characters more flexibly.

Text formatted as strings can be displayed on a graphical view with the usual onDraw() method along with other shapes. It uses a canvas method like these other shapes, which is

canvas.drawText()

This takes four parameters. The first is the string variable or a constant literal value. Then there are two position values for the x and y points at which the string is to be displayed. As usual, these represent the top left corner, this time of the text. Finally, it needs a paint object.

The paint object allows us to start printing at a precise position and it gives us access to all the usual paint properties and methods, such as,

paint.setColor(Color.WHITE)

as well as text-specific methods, such as

paint.setTextSize(16)

or, paint.setTextSize(w /12),

which would set the character size to one twelfth of the screen width.

The GameView Constructor

The constructor has to initialize all the variables listed in the attributes, except paint which is already initialized. The code is,

```
public GameView(Context context) {
    super(context);
    w = getResources().getDisplayMetrics().widthPixels;
    h = getResources().getDisplayMetrics().heightPixels;
    int background = Color.rgb(20, 40, 60);
    setBackgroundColor(background);
    c=Color.rgb(200, 140, 80);
    figure = new Figure(w/4, w/2, h/2, c, Color.WHITE);
    heading =" Get the Ball";
    message1 ="other team has the ball";
    message2 = "try to get it from them";
    message3 = " touch to start";
    paint = new Paint();
    setOnTouchListener(this);
}
```

There is nothing very new about this code, but we have added statements to set a couple of colors including one for the sprite face and another for a dark background. We have also used setOnTouchListener() as required for our onTouch() method.

We have also initialized the text strings to appropriate values. The value of the heading variable is set to "Get the Ball" which is a more instructive expansion of the app name– although it will still be formally identified as Getball in the device and the Play Store. Leter we will make an adjustment to display the same name on the app icon. The heading string starts with two blank characters as a simple way of centering the heading on the screen by shifting it slightly to the right.

The other messages are user instructions as illustrated in Figure 1.

The onDraw() Method

To get the display shown in Figure 1 we use the onDraw() method. This sets the color to white to show clearly against the dark background. The text size is set to w/12 so it is scaled to the device screen and the text strings are also positioned relative to the screen.

Here we have to experiment to get a reasonable layout. So the position coordinates are all relative to w and h and were obtained by trial and error.

The code draws the heading and two messages then draws the figure object, then adds the scores and the message to touch the screen to advance to the game action.

The score and best score are drawn by concatenating string constants with the variables, score and best, to draw the outputs as strings.

```
public void onDraw(Canvas canvas) {
    paint.setColor(Color.WHITE);
    paint.setTextSize(w /12);
    canvas.drawText(heading, w/4, h/6, paint);
    paint.setTextSize(w / 20);
    canvas.drawText(message1, w/4, 6*h/20, paint);
    canvas.drawText(message2, w/4, 7*h/20, paint);
    figure.draw(canvas);
canvas.drawText("Current score is "+score, 3*w/10, 13*h/20, paint);
canvas.drawText("  Best score is "+best, 3*w/10, 14*h/20, paint);
```

```
paint.setColor(Color.YELLOW);
canvas.drawText(message3, w/4, 18 * h / 20, paint);
}
```

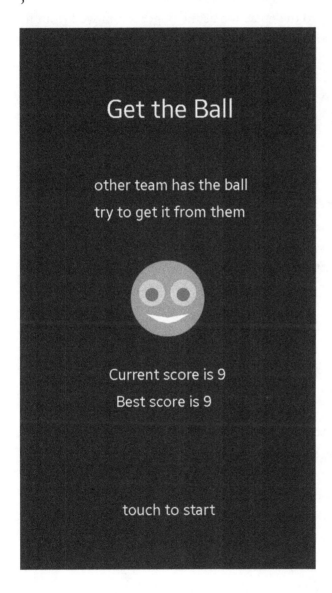

Figure 1. The introductory screen for the final app.

The onTouch() Method

The method is a very simple one. It responds to a touch anywhere on the view and only to the up action as the finger is removed from the screen. This avoids multiple or long touches and generates only one event. So when the touch ends a number of actions are carried out.

First the contentView is set to shapeView where the action takes place. Then the score is set to 0 so that if a game has already taken place it restarts at 0.

Then it starts the timer which you may recall was stopped in the previous app when the player collided with a sprite.

Of course, there is no startTimer method yet so we will have to do something about that. Then it calls the shapeView setup() method which resets all the parameters for another action.

The code is

```
public boolean onTouch(View v, MotionEvent event) {

    if (event.getAction() == MotionEvent.ACTION_UP) {
      setContentView(shapeView);
      score=0;
      shapeView.startTimer();
      shapeView.setup();
    }
    return true;
}
```

The ShapeView Class

This is already written and is a straight copy from the Faces app but it needs some modifications to record the scores and work with the gameView screen.

The main change is to remove the timer code from the constructor and locate it in a separate function, startTimer(). This is required because the timer is stopped when the player collides with a sprite to end the game. The idea is to return the player to gameView to display the scores then allow it to be restarted by calling timerStart() from gameView. So the action is now started from gameView instead of the shapeView constructor when the objects are being created.

In that case, we might do the same for setup(), that is, call it from gameView instead of shapeView. So we remove the call to setup() from the ShapeView constructor and now we have both shapeView.startTimer and shapeView.setup() called from gameView when the touch event starts the game.

There is one other modification we can now make that should make the game more interesting. This is to reduce the time interval of the timer after each ball is collected. Then the game will get faster and faster are more balls are collected until it becomes too fast to handle and the game ends.

We can do this by replacing the constant 40 in the timer code by a variable, t. Then t will be added to the instance variables and initialized to 40 in the constructor. Since it is visible to all the shapeView methods we can decrement it as each ball is collected. We can also reset t to 40 in gameView when the touch event starts the game.

The Collect() Method

Apart from startTimer() only two other changes are required to ShapeView. The first is to collect() and the second is to onDraw().

The collect() method now has to increment the value of score decrement the value of the time parameter t and store the value of score in the variable, best, if it is better than the existing value. Then having changed the value of t it has to stop the counter and start it again with the new value. This is the only way to reset the timer. So the code is

```
private void collect(){
    if (Math.abs(ball.x - figure.x) < size / 2 &&
            Math.abs(ball.y - figure.y) < size / 2) {
        float x= (float)(size/2+Math.random()*(w-size));
        float y=(float)(size/2+Math.random()*(h-4*size));
        ball= new Ball(size, x, y);
        score++;
        if(t>4)t-=2;
        if(score>best)best=score;
        timer.cancel();
        startTimer();
    }
}
```

The onDraw() Method

This only requires the addition of a running score readout and the best score. These can be added to the bottom of the screen but, of course, we now have to add a paint object to the ShapeView attributes since we will need to use it here.

```
public void onDraw(Canvas canvas) {
    paint.setColor(Color.WHITE);
    ball.draw(canvas);
    paint.setTextSize(w /20);
    canvas.drawText("score", 10, h-size, paint);
    canvas.drawText("best", w-size, h-size, paint);
    canvas.drawText(" "+score, 10, h-size/2, paint);
    canvas.drawText(" "+best, w-size, h-size/2, paint);
    for (int i = 0; i < sprite.length; i++) {
        sprite[i].draw(canvas);
    }
    figure.draw(canvas);
}
```

We set the text size and the color then add "score" in the bottom left corner and "best" in the bottom right corner. This requires some scaled positioning to get them in the right places. Then we print the values of the variables, score and best below the text. This time we cheat a little by concatenating the varaibles with blank strings so they appear by themselves.

The Full Java Code

For what we have done so far the code is as follows and the outcome is as illustrated in Figure 2.

```
package com.androidjavaapps.ballgetter;

import android.os.*;
import android.app.*;
import android.view.*;
import android.content.*;
import android.graphics.*;
import java.util.*;
import android.view.View.*;

public class MainActivity extends Activity {
```

```
    ShapeView shapeView;
    GameView gameView;
    int score=0, best=0;

    @Override
    protected void onCreate(Bundle savedInstanceState) {
        super.onCreate(savedInstanceState);
        this.requestWindowFeature(Window.FEATURE_NO_TITLE);
        getWindow().setFlags(WindowManager.LayoutParams.
            FLAG_FULLSCREEN,
WindowManager.LayoutParams.FLAG_FULLSCREEN);
        shapeView=new ShapeView(this);
        gameView=new GameView(this);
        setContentView(gameView);
        score=0;
        best=0;
    }

    public class GameView extends View implements
OnTouchListener{
        float w, h;
        int c, ch;
        Figure figure;
        String heading, message1, message2, message3, message4;
        Paint paint;

        public GameView(Context context) {
            super(context);
            w = getResources().getDisplayMetrics().widthPixels;
            h = getResources().getDisplayMetrics().heightPixels;
            int background = Color.rgb(20, 40, 60);
            setBackgroundColor(background);
            c=Color.rgb(200, 140, 80);
            figure = new Figure(w/4, w/2, h/2, c, Color.WHITE);
            heading ="Get the Ball";
            message1 ="other team has the ball";
            message2 = "try to get it from them";
            message3 = " touch to start";
```

```java
        paint = new Paint();
        setOnTouchListener(this);
    }


    public void onDraw(Canvas canvas) {
        paint.setColor(Color.WHITE);
        paint.setTextSize(w / 12);
        canvas.drawText(heading, w/4, h/6, paint);
        paint.setTextSize(w / 20);
        canvas.drawText(message1, w/4, 6*h/20, paint);
        canvas.drawText(message2, w/4, 7*h/20, paint);
        figure.draw(canvas);
    canvas.drawText("Current score is " + score, 3*w/10, 13*h/20,
paint);
    canvas.drawText(" Best score is " + best, 3*w/10, 14*h/20, paint);
        paint.setColor(Color.YELLOW);
        canvas.drawText(message3, w / 3, 18 * h / 20, paint);
    }


    public boolean onTouch(View v, MotionEvent event) {
        if (event.getAction() == MotionEvent.ACTION_UP) {
            setContentView(shapeView);
            score=0;
            shapeView.startTimer();
            shapeView.setup();
        }
        return true;
    }
}



    public class ShapeView extends View implements
OnTouchListener{
        Sprite[] sprite;
        Figure figure;
        Timer timer;
        float w, h, size;
        int c, ch;
        Paint paint;
```

```
int found=0;
Ball ball;
int t;

public ShapeView(Context context){
   super(context);
   w=getResources().getDisplayMetrics().widthPixels;
   h=getResources().getDisplayMetrics().heightPixels;
   d = getResources().getDisplayMetrics().densityDpi;
   size=d/2;
   int elements=Math.round(w*h/(size*size*9));
   int background=Color.rgb(40, 50, 60);
   setBackgroundColor(background);
   sprite = new Sprite[elements];
   paint = new Paint();
   setOnTouchListener(this);
   t=40;
}

private void startTimer(){
   timer=new Timer();
   timer.schedule(new TimerTask(){
   public void run(){
      runOnUiThread(new Runnable(){
         @Override
         public void run() {
            move();
            invalidate(); //after they have all moved
         }
         });
      }
},0,t);
}

public void setup(){
   boolean separated=true;
   double direction;
   float x, y, vx, vy, vxMax=3, vyMax=3;
   c=Color.rgb(100,150,250);
```

```
        ch=Color.rgb(200, 140, 80);
        figure = new Figure(size, w/2, h-size/2, ch, Color.WHITE);
        for (int i=0; i<sprite.length; i++){
            x= (float)(size/2+Math.random()*(w-size));
            y=(float)(size/2+Math.random()*(h-3*size));
            vx=(float) Math.random()*vxMax+1;
            direction= Math.random()-0.5;
            if(direction<0)vx=-vx; // to get negative directions
            vy=(float) Math.random()*vyMax+1;
            direction= Math.random()-0.5;
            if(direction<0)vy=-vy;
            separated = checkSeparation(size, x,y,i);
            if(separated == true) sprite[i]=new Sprite(size, x,
y,c,Color.WHITE,vx,vy);
            else i--;
        }
        x= (float)(size/2+Math.random()*(w-size));
        y=(float)(size/2+Math.random()*(h-4*size));
        ball = new Ball(size, x, y);
    }

    private void move(){
        for(int i=0;i<sprite.length;i++){
        sprite[i].count++;   // increment sprite frame
        sprite[i].x+=sprite[i].vx;
        sprite[i].y+=sprite[i].vy;
        reflect(i);
        bounce(i);
        checkCollision(i);
        collect();
        }
    }

    private void collect(){
        if (Math.abs(ball.x - figure.x) < size / 2 &&
            Math.abs(ball.y - figure.y) < size / 2) {
        float x= (float)(size/2+Math.random()*(w-size));
        float y=(float)(size/2+Math.random()*(h-4*size));
        ball= new Ball(size, x, y);
```

```
        score++;
        if(t>4)t-=2;
        if(score>best)best=score;
        timer.cancel();
        startTimer();
      }
   }

private boolean checkSeparation(float size, float x, float y, int i){
    float sepX, sepY;
    for(int j=0; j<i; j++){
       sepX=Math.abs(x-sprite[j].x);
       sepY=Math.abs(y-sprite[j].y);
       if(sepX<size && sepY<size) return false;
    }
    return true;
}

  private void checkCollision(int j){
     float sepX, sepY;
     sepX=Math.abs(figure.x-sprite[j].x);
     sepY=Math.abs(figure.y-sprite[j].y);
     if(Math.sqrt(sepX*sepX+sepY*sepY)<size) {
        timer.cancel();
        t=40;
        setContentView(gameView);
     }
  }

  public void onDraw(Canvas canvas) {
     paint.setColor(Color.WHITE);
     coin.draw(canvas);
     paint.setTextSize(w /20);
     canvas.drawText("score", 10, h-size, paint);
     canvas.drawText("best", w-size, h-size, paint);
     canvas.drawText(" "+score, 10, h-size/2, paint);
     canvas.drawText(" "+best, w-size, h-size/2, paint);
     for (int i = 0; i < sprite.length; i++) {
        sprite[i].draw(canvas);
```

```
      }
      figure.draw(canvas);
   }

   private void reflect(int i) {
      if (sprite[i].x < size / 2) {
         sprite[i].x = size / 2;
         sprite[i].vx = -sprite[i].vx;
      }
      if (sprite[i].x > w - size / 2) {
         sprite[i].x = w - size / 2;
         sprite[i].vx = -sprite[i].vx;
      }
      if (sprite[i].y < size/2) {
         sprite[i].y = size/2;
         sprite[i].vy = -sprite[i].vy;
      }
      if (sprite[i].y > h - size/2) {
         sprite[i].y = h - size/2;
         sprite[i].vy = -sprite[i].vy;
      }
   }

   private void bounce(int i){
      float tempvx, tempvy;
      double sep, sepX, sepY;
      for(int j=i+1; j<sprite.length; j++){
         sepX = Math.abs(sprite[i].x-sprite[j].x);
         sepY = Math.abs(sprite[i].y-sprite[j].y);
         sep=Math.sqrt(sepX*sepX + sepY*sepY);
         if(sep<=size) {
            tempvx=sprite[i].vx;
            tempvy=sprite[i].vy;
            sprite[i].vx=sprite[j].vx;
            sprite[i].vy=sprite[j].vy;
            sprite[j].vx=tempvx;
            sprite[j].vy=tempvy;
            sprite[i].x+=sprite[i].vx;
            sprite[i].y+=sprite[i].vy;
```

```
                sprite[j].x+=sprite[j].vx;
                sprite[j].y+=sprite[j].vy;
            }
        }
    }

    public boolean onTouch(View v, MotionEvent event){
        float px, py, pr;
        float x = event.getRawX();
        float y = event.getRawY();

        switch (event.getAction()){
            case MotionEvent.ACTION_DOWN:
                px=figure.x;
                py=figure.y;
                pr=size/2;
                if (x<px+pr&&x>px-pr&& y<py+pr&&y>py-pr){
                    figure.x=x;
                    figure.y=y;
                    found=1;
                    return true;
                }
                break;
            case MotionEvent.ACTION_MOVE:
                if(found>0){
                    figure.x=x;
                    figure.y=y;
                }
                break;
            case MotionEvent.ACTION_UP:
                found=0;
                break;

            default:
        }
        invalidate();
        return true;
    }
}
```

}

Figure 2. The Getball app.

What Next

We now have a more or less complete app that can be modified further to get your own version. The app can be downloaded from the Play Store.

The only finishing touches required are to have a look at some of the other files in the app.

14. Publication

The Aim

The aim now is to complete the production of the final app and prepare it for publication on the Google Play Store.

First we can have a look at some of the other files that make up the app and modify some of them. These are all XML files but there is really not much need to understand XML. Basically it is a text method of representing data that is widely used in all sorts of computer applications. It is similar to the HTML used in web pages.

In this case, as for HTML, it defines a user interface as a hierarchy of tags containing other tags and attributes. The file is always written entirely in lower case (unless some object names are included) and often starts with some sort of declaration stating the version of XML that is used.

The Manifest File

This is the main XML file that defines the general parameters of the app. It starts with a declaration starting with <? then has a lot of text

content enclosed in an opening <manifest> and a closing </manifest> tag.

The opening tag has a couple of attributes inside the pair of angle brackets < and > then a nested <application> </application> tag pair. This too has some attributes inside the opening tag then an <activity> </activity> pair, and so on, to describe the hierarchy of tags.

The first attribute of the manifest tag defines the xml namespace, xmlns:android, which looks like a web address but is actually just a namespace-like a folder. The other is the package name of the application, in this case, com.androidjavaapps.ballgetter. Both of these values are enclosed in quotation marks.

The other attributes in the document are also name and value pairs where the value is always a text string. In general, an XML file may also contain a string value between the tags which are called text nodes and not enclosed in quotes. This particular document does not have any examples of text nodes.

So the manifest files is

```
<?xml version="1.0" encoding="utf-8"?>
<manifest
xmlns:android="http://schemas.android.com/apk/res/android"
 package="com.androidjavaapps.runner" >

    <application
      android:allowBackup="true"
      android:icon="@drawable/ic_launcher"
      android:label="@string/app_name"
      android:theme="@style/AppTheme" >
      <activity
```

```
        android:name=".MainActivity"
        android:label="@string/app_name" >
        <intent-filter>
            <action android:name="android.intent.action.MAIN" />
            <category
    android:name="android.intent.category.LAUNCHER" />
        </intent-filter>
    </activity>
  </application>
</manifest>
```

We can edit the line,

android:icon="@drawable/ic_launcher", to

android:icon="@drawable/face".

This will replace the launcher icon file with a new one called face.

Then we can create a png file called face (all lower case since it is going into an XML document). Preferably we should make it a png with a transparent background. And save it in the @drawable folder.

When the app is recompiled it will use this file instead of the default ic_launcher file and display the new launcher icon as illustrated in Figure 1.

Figure 1. The redesigned Getball icon.

The Screen Orientation Problem

At last we can deal with the problem of the app restarting when the device is rotated from portrait to landscape orientation. There are two ways to handle this. One is to save all the current game parameters in a Bundle object and read these when the app restarts by running the onCreate() method. If you want to let your users rotate to landscape mode then this is the way forward.

The simpler alternative and the approach adopted here is to stop the app responding to reorientation. We can do this by adding a single line to the manifest file as an additional attribute at the end of the <activity> attributes. It must be inserted before the closing > of the <activity> tag as follows,

```
<activity
    android:name=".MainActivity"
    android:label="@string/app_name"
    android:screenOrientation="portrait">

    <intent-filter>
      <action android:name="android.intent.action.MAIN" />
      <category
android:name="android.intent.category.LAUNCHER" />
    </intent-filter>

</activity>
```

Now the app will always stay in portrait mode.

The Layout File

This is another XML file, which is generally used to define the layout of the app. We have not used this approach since the entire app has been coded in Java, including the layout. The XML defines a static layout and is very good at it but our requirement was for a dynamic layout which is best achieved with code. Anyway, for information, the default layout file is

```
<RelativeLayout
xmlns:android="http://schemas.android.com/apk/res/android"
   xmlns:tools="http://schemas.android.com/tools"
android:layout_width="match_parent"
   android:layout_height="match_parent"
android:paddingLeft="@dimen/activity_horizontal_margin"
   android:paddingRight="@dimen/activity_horizontal_margin"
   android:paddingTop="@dimen/activity_vertical_margin"
   android:paddingBottom="@dimen/activity_vertical_margin"
tools:context=".MainActivity">
   <TextView android:text="@string/hello_world"
android:layout_width="wrap_content"
      android:layout_height="wrap_content" />
</RelativeLayout>
```

Again, it is a recognizable hierarchy of nested XML tags with attributes.

The Strings File

```
<?xml version="1.0" encoding="utf-8"?>
<resources>
   <string name="app_name">Get Ball</string>
```

```
<string name="hello_world">Hello world!</string>
<string name="action_settings">Settings</string>
</resources>
```

This is another XML file which contains any string data used in the app. In fact we only use the first two lines but it does no harm to keep the entire file. However, we can change the string "Get Ball" to anything else we like. This will rename the title of our app as displayed with the launch icon. We will keep it for our app but you might like to change it for yours. In fact, Get Ball is too generic to show up in a Play Store search so it is best to change it.

Preparing for Publication

The apps we have been producing work very well in our Android devices and in those of anyone else who cares to copy them. However they will not be accepted by the Play Store or any other app publisher in their present form. Each app is called app-debug.apk. This is a debug version with extra code that is required for testing and debugging which has to be removed.

The app also has to be published with a certificate that has the developer's unique key. So far, our apps are running under temporary keys provided by Android Studio. All software applications require certificates with public keys that identify the developers and the same is true for publication in the Google Play Store.

So we have to produce a final release version of the app that is stripped of superfluous code and properly certificated. You can do this in Android Studio by clicking the Build tab from the top tool bar and Generate Signed APK … which opens the window shown in Figure 1.

Figure 1. The Wizard to generate a signed apk file.

You can leave the form blank and just click Create new… to open the New Key Store window as in Figure 2.

Figure 2. The New Key Store window.

Now you can click the … button on the right of the form to browse your folders and select one for your key file as shown in Figure 3.

Figure 3. The Project Folder.

Then just type in a file name. For example you might use Keystore to create a Keystore.jks file in the projects folder.

Then OK returns you to the previous window where you can enter the password details and personal details if you want, then click Next to return to the IDE.

Now when you click Run to run the app, Studio will produce a signed release version. However, it will not run it. The apk file is saved in the BallGetter/App folder as a new file, app-release.apk. This is the file you can upload to the Play Store.

To run it on your device you have to copy the file to the device then find the file and tap its name. You will be invited to use the app installer to install it on your device.

If you want to go on developing the app or to add an update then you should revert to the debug version to test the app directly in the AVD or the attached device.

Getting a Google Account

To publish apps on the Google Play Store you must register for a Google Play Developer account. You can do this on the Google website at

https://support.google.com/googleplay/android-developer

You will have to pay Google a one-off registration fee, currently at $25, and to do this you will have to sign up for a Google Wallet account. All of these processes can be implemented at the website and are very well explained.

Publishing the App

The publication process is explained fully on the Android Developer site at

http://developer.android.com/tools/publishing/preparing.html

There is also a useful launch checklist at

http://developer.android.com/distribute/tools/launch-checklist.html

Basically you need to go through the following processes:-

- Prepare a release version of the app as outlined above signed with your own certification key.

- Get a Google Play Developer account as described above.

- Prepare promotional materials which must include graphic files and a description of your app.

- Upload the release version of the apk file and the promotional materials to the Google Play developer site at

http://developer.android.com/distribute/googleplay/start.html

Promotional Materials

To promote your app on the Play Store you have to provide a high resolution, 512 by 512 pixel image of the launcher icon. It has to be a transparent png file. You will have to find a suitable graphics package to produce this. The image shown in Figure 5, for example, was produced with Adobe Flash. You can also use Microsoft's PowerPoint with a page size of about 13.54 by 13.54. There are many other free graphics packages available that you can use provided they save transparent png files. As a last resort you can write your own Figure app to draw a suitable icon and save the screenshot from your Android device.

Figure 5. The high resolution icon.

You are also asked for a description of the app. This serves to inform the reader and is also used by the Play Store search engine so you should take the opportunity to include as many relevant keywords as possible to help users to find your app. You should also upload some image files to illustrate your app. Of course, all of these materials should be prepared beforehand.

The other graphics can be screenshots from the app itself. You can get these by running the app in your Android device then pressing a button combination to save the current screen image. The actual buttons vary from one device to another and can be discovered in a web search. They are usually a combination of two keys from the power key, the home key, the back button, and the sound volume button. In fact you are asked for screenshots from a range of devices but you can just upload whatever you have got.

The screenshot file is saved as a png file in a Pictures or Screenshots folder somewhere in the files of your device and can be transferred by USB or cloud repository to a PC for upload to the developer website.

The Google Developer Console

If you go to the Google Developer Console you will have to login with your username and password. You are presented with an option to add a new app then a page that requires the promotional information described above before you are able to upload the release version of your app. The information required should be prepared beforehand and is

Title [30 characters]

The name of your app in 30 characters or less including spaces.

Short description [80]

A short description of your app in 80 characters or less, including spaces.

Full description [4000]

A description of the app in 4000 characters. This should include all the important keywords to help Play Store users to find your app.

Graphic assets

- Screenshots of your app. You must upload at least 2 and no more than 8 jpeg or png files with no alpha channel (that is no transparent background). You should upload separate examples for a phone, 7 inch tablet, 10 inch tablet and TV screen if you have them.

- A high resolution image of your icon. It should be a 512 by 512 image in a png file with an alpha channel if possible. That means a transparent background

- A feature graphic in the form of a 1024 by 500 jpg or png with no alpha.

- A promo graphic which is a small icon file, 180 by 120, 24 bit jpg or png with no alpha.

- A TV listing if you have one.

- A promo video from YouTube if you have one.

Categorization

You have to complete a form that puts your app in a category indicating its suitability for various users, especially children.

Contact details

You have to provide a website URL and an email contact address. You can also enter a phone number for user contact.

Privacy policy

You can specify a privacy policy if your app is likely to affect the user's privacy.

What Next

The idea now is that you should be able to produce your own game app and publish it in the Play Store. You can use any of the apps developed in this book and modify them any way you want.

You should also take care to use your own package name or the app may conflict with others on the Play Store. You should also choose you own name for the app. Get Ball is not very imaginative.

One aim of the book has been to help you to write your own app but a more important aim has been to help you to find out if you enjoy programming.

If you are reading this you have probably done exactly that. So welcome to the club.

Index

About the Author

Bill Tait is a physicist with a PhD in Nuclear Physics but he has spent most of his career teaching computing to undergraduates. He has published one other book on Radiation Detection and another entitled Start Programming with JavaScript. He has published educational software, some written in JavaScript, as well as a few Android apps. He also has an interest in website design and online learning, on which subject he has published a number of research papers. His website is at www.billtait.com.

www.ingramcontent.com/pod-product-compliance
Lightning Source LLC
Chambersburg PA
CBHW071417050326
40689CB00010B/1883